FINDING YOUR WAY

NAVIGATIONAL TOOLS FOR INTERNATIONAL STUDENT AND SCHOLAR ADVISERS

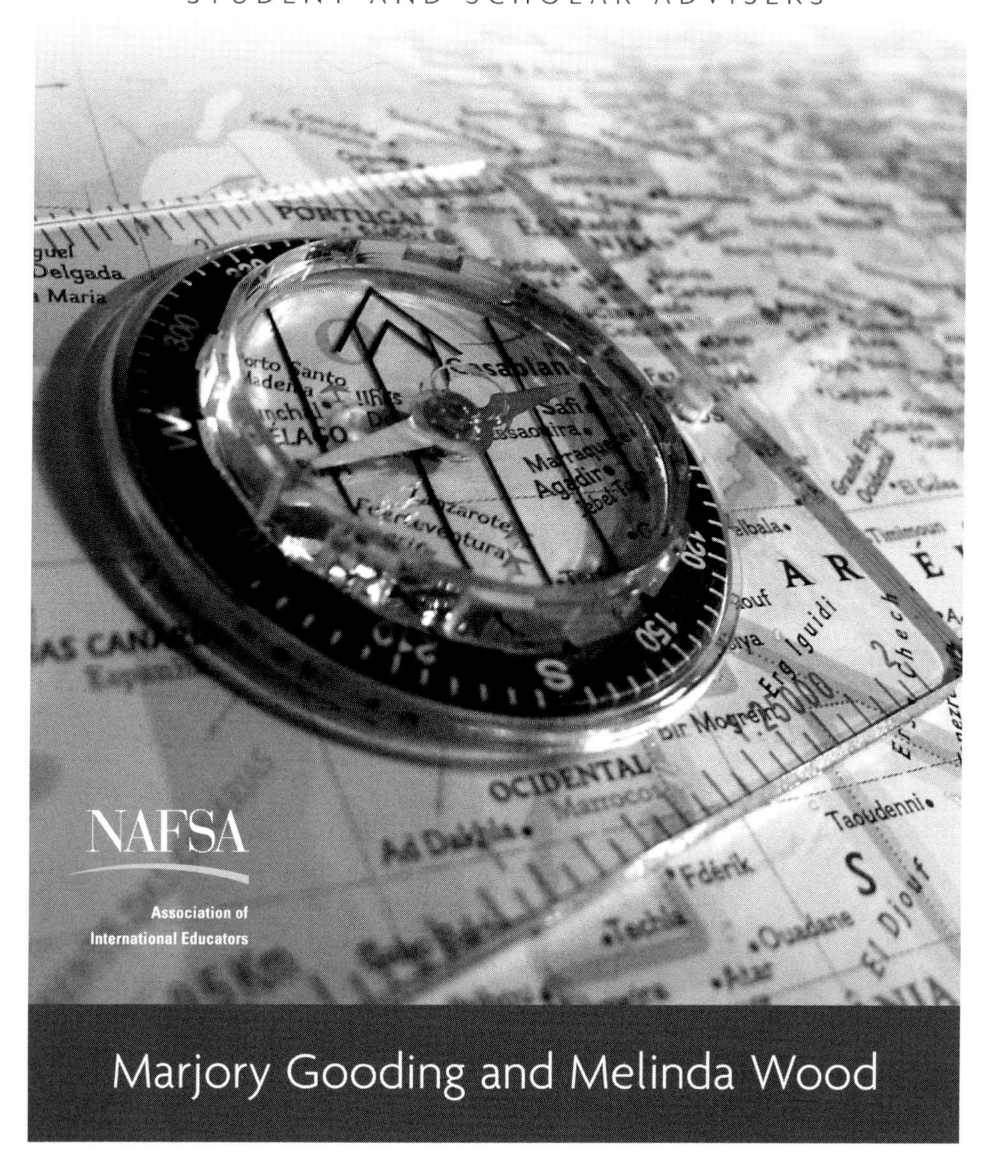

Marjory Gooding and Melinda Wood

NAFSA: Association of International Educators is an association of individuals worldwide advancing international education and exchange. NAFSA serves its members, their institutions and organizations, and others engaged in international education and exchange and global workforce development. NAFSA sets and upholds standards of good practice; provides training, professional development, and networking opportunities; and advocates for international education.

Printed in the United States of America.

Editor: Jan Steiner, NAFSA
Inside Design and Production: Drew Banks, NAFSA
Cover Design: Larnish & Associates

Library of Congress Cataloging-in-Publication Data

Gooding, Marjory.

Finding your way: navigational tools for international student and scholar advisers / Marjory Gooding and Melinda Wood.

p. cm.

Includes bibliographical references.

ISBN 0-912207-90-6 (alk. paper)

1. Educational counseling. 2. Students, Foreign—United States. 3. Educational counseling—Vocational guidance. I. Wood, Melinda. II. Title.

LB1027.5.G585 2006

371.4—dc22

2006048187

TABLE OF CONTENTS

TABLE OF CONTENTS

APPENDIXES

Preface

When we first decided to write this book, we grappled with the essential question of how we could best help new international student and scholar advisers jump-start their careers. New advisers have a pressing need for practical advice and information that can help them on a daily basis, but they also need to frame their day-to-day issues in the broader historical and theoretical contexts that shape the profession. We realize that the latter may not be terribly interesting to new advisers, so we have tried to mix up the practical and theoretical sections and to interject real-life examples of how theory and practice intersect.

How to Use This Book

We know that not everyone likes to read from front to back. This book does not need to be used sequentially, although there is some inherent sense in doing so. You may want to skim the whole book before doing any of the chapter follow-up activities that will help you build your skills in each area. Whatever you decide, we recommend that you do the activities in small increments as your schedule allows. It could take a year or more to complete the activities and years more to continue refining them. In Appendix D, we have consolidated all of the activities into a master list that begins with small, safe actions for you to take and ends with more complex activities that skilled advisers should be willing and able to take. It will be helpful to go back periodically and reread sections to make sure you are becoming a strategic professional in international education, not just a survivor adviser.

Disclaimer

This book is not a 21st century version of Gary Althen's seminal work, *The Handbook of Foreign Student Advising*, first published in 1984 and revised in 1995. While we owe a debt to Gary for first conceptualizing a single volume, easy-to-use guide for international student advisers, we also acknowledge that the context in which new advisers are entering the profession has changed dramatically in the past ten years. Higher education in the United States is operating under some radically changed assumptions, the role of the United States in global politics has changed, and the people who are just now entering the profession are not necessarily drawn to it for the same reasons that their predecessors were.

Acknowledgments

Thanks to our friends, families, and colleagues who encouraged and enabled us in this project. Special thanks go to the following people who read early versions of the manuscript and shared their invaluable feedback: Laura Flower Kim, Joedy Hu, Becky George, Jane Kalionzes, and Tina Tan. We also acknowledge the many colleagues we have enjoyed over our careers: those who mentored us, guided us in our professional development, and showed us examples of what not to do as well as what we should do. NAFSA: Association of International Educators has given us many opportunities to test our own strategic thinking and skill building in our volunteer roles as trainers and leaders at various levels. NAFSA has been an excellent source of support and guidance. We look forward to observing the emerging leadership of those new professionals who are entering the exciting field of international student and scholar advising.

ABOUT THE AUTHORS

About Marjory Gooding

Marjory Gooding has worked and learned along her nineteen year route in international education at the University of Colorado at Boulder, the Massachusetts Institute of Technology, and the California Institute of Technology. She has served on a number of NAFSA committees focusing on regulatory matters, advocacy, and publications. Previously she taught art history and architectural history, where her interest in art and the people who create it paved the way to a passionate interest in the people she works with and a critical mindset for reading the law. Her two amazing daughters taught her much of what she needed to know about career planning so that she and Melinda Wood could write this book.

About Melinda Wood

Melinda Wood has been an intrepid sojourner in the world of international education for more than 30 years, having taught ESL, coordinated a homestay program, advised international students and scholars, and prepared employment-based visa applications in a human resources office along the way. She has held a variety of member leadership positions in NAFSA and in other nonprofit organizations. Melinda has a Ph.D. in higher education administration and currently works in Academic Affairs at the University of Hawaii–West Oahu. She has learned to keep her navigational tools in good working order so that she can always find her way to the next great opportunity.

GETTING STARTED

CHAPTER 1

Introduction

Welcome to the exciting field of international advising!

We hope that you are going to enjoy this fascinating work as much as we do. A large part of our rationale for writing this book is to provide some insights and the practical tools that will help you to succeed while reducing some of the frustration that comes with starting a challenging and multifaceted position. But first, some general background on the field of international education overall will help.

International education in colleges and universities usually is composed of several somewhat autonomous components: advising inbound students and scholars, advising outbound students, establishing academic agreements and partnerships, teaching English as a Second Language (ESL), administering ESL programs, dealing with regulations, providing programs and community linkages, and more. What you are doing is just one piece in a large mosaic of activities that make up the field. And these activities are embedded in the much bigger picture of higher education, internationalization, and globalization.

The profession of international advising in the United States was launched in the early twentieth century as the numbers of students seeking an American higher education increased (Glazier and Kenschaft 2002; Merkx 2003). Both World Wars I and II were pivotal events in shaping how the U.S. government, as well as individual institutions, responded to the flow of students coming to the United States (Mestenhauser 1997). The profession took its first formal steps toward recognition in 1948 when the National Association of Foreign Student Advisers was formed. Over the years, the organization evolved to better represent the complexities of the profession, first changing its name to National Association for Foreign Student Affairs (1964) in an attempt to be more inclusive of other professionals who work with international students such as ESL program administrators and admissions counselors. Then terminologies changed along with the work; and to accommodate those who deal with students who go abroad for an educational experience and those who help the international academic workforce (professors, researchers, and other scholars) to enter the United States, NAFSA became a "word," not an acronym, and the official name of the organization became NAFSA: Association of International Educators in 1990.

Recognizing this complexity ourselves, we struggled with word choices in describing this slice of the profession often called international *student* advising. In fact, a good percentage of those who advise international students also provide services to a diverse group of international academics who participate in "knowledge production" rather than "knowledge consumption" (students). Members of this group include postdoctoral scholars, researchers, instructors, doctors in human and veterinary medicine, and tenure-track professors. Within the field, these academics are generally described as *scholars*. One commonly accepted title for advisers who serve the spectrum of incoming populations is *international student and scholar adviser.* However, some advisers work with only one group or the other, so this title does not fit their particular position. After much discussion, we decided to use the term *international adviser* in this book. We realize some people may not agree with our use of the term, but we believe it is sufficiently generic to encompass the professional work that universities and colleges provide to assist people from other countries who want to have official interactions with those institutions.

The scope of this book is limited to the development of the profession in the United States, but we hope that international advisers in other countries will find it useful by modifying the specifics to fit their particular institutional, national, and cultural context. We do not presume to understand the workings of other countries' governmental policies or how administrative work is organized in colleges and universities around the world; some days we barely understand our own systems!

During the 1970s and 1980s, the number of international students coming to the United States increased steeply. New hires in international education were expected to have a vaguely amorphous combination of experiences, traits, and predispositions such as overseas living, foreign language ability, interest in other cultures, enthusiasm, and high energy. Most of the specific professional skills were learned on the job under the guidance of more senior staff, that is, if the newcomer was lucky. Many senior professionals in international education today recall their first day on the job when they walked into an empty office with a couple of outdated reference manuals and were told, "You're on your own now!" Teaching ESL may be the exception, though horror stories of new teachers being dropped solo into schools (we use the term advisedly) around the world abound.

Fortunately, as a new adviser to international students and scholars, you have much better resources and opportunities for learning your job. At the end of this chapter you will find several activities to help you start identifying them.

It is fair to say that the world of work, and specifically work in international education, has become increasingly complex. No one can expect to succeed, much less thrive, simply by mastering the tasks of the job. It may be hard to imagine that some people at your institution will not share your excitement about listening to voices speak with unfamiliar accents, smelling the aromatic scents of unknown foods, and learning the finer points of cricket, say, instead of baseball. Nor can you expect to stay in your current job indefinitely; as universities and colleges are required to be more accountable to governing boards and/or the public, your career may take some unanticipated twists and turns. Add to that the likelihood that your values or interests may change over time, and you realize that the road ahead may not be so clear.

We know that you need to master a lot of technical skills and knowledge to be a good international adviser—and you will. At the same time, we know that it is easy to get lost in the details and not remember to look at the bigger picture. We believe that is no longer enough simply for a "good" adviser to know the regulations and love international students. To be a pro-active, career-shaping, twenty-first century professional in higher education, we believe you absolutely must 1) develop your political acumen, 2) understand how your institution works and where you fit in it, 3) learn how to think strategically for your unit and yourself, and 4) know your own values and limits. This book will help you to connect your day-to-day tasks with these higher order responsibilities. By providing the necessary background and tools to do so, we want you to become an *excellent* adviser and an indispensable asset for your campus and community.

Career Path Research

In the past thirty years, theories of career development have evolved and have been widely adopted by university and college career service centers. One popular framework for examining career development focuses on the relationship between the individual and the environment. Holland (1973) was one of the early proponents of this approach. He developed a classification system that matched types of personal characteristics and interests with types of environments to identify vocational preferences. A similar typology is the Strong Interest Inventory® (Strong 1922), a self-assessment tool significantly expanded in the 1970s and still widely used. The Meyers-Briggs Type Inventory® (MBTI) (Myers and Briggs 1940) is another instrument that also has been applied to work settings and used by both of us in various jobs we have held.

Another school of career development theories draws on stage-based theories of individual development. Life stage theories contend that there is a progression of challenges, such as intellectual, interpersonal, or moral concerns, which must be worked out at set times during the lifespan. These stages can also be discerned in the challenges that occur over a career and can lead to various career decisions and paths (Kegan 1982).

More recently, Bloch (2005, p. 195) has proposed a systems approach in which a career is viewed as a "complex adaptive entity" that operates within many networks rather than along only the two dimensions of personality and work setting. Features of this approach include reinventing while moving across and within networks to maintain balance among components such as work, leisure, family, and so on. Perhaps because international advising offers multiple paths for entering the field and growing from within our positions, Bloch's comment rings true, "People experience parts of their careers that seem to form patterns for them, but these patterns are either not explicable, or are only partially explained, in terms of the patterns of other careers. The career development of each individual is a series of choices that have internal harmonics or resonances for that individual and can only be understood in terms of that individual" (Bloch 2005, p. 200).

International Education Career Path Research

The work of international advisers has not been the subject of a great deal of scholarly research. A study in 1984 by Millett-Sorensen and Crownhart examined the influence of international advisers in their institutions. They surveyed 800 international advisers (485 respondents, 61 percent) and found that less than half worked full-time. These advisers held a variety of academic degrees, were mostly female, and enjoyed their work with students of different nationalities but felt that the position of international adviser was one of the least influential positions on their campuses.

More recently, Rosser et al. (forthcoming 2007) conducted a national study that focused primarily on the impact of SEVIS on advisers' worklives. With a response rate of 45 percent (more than 1,200 respondents), the study provides a comprehensive profile of U.S. international advisers today. The field is still overwhelmingly female (nearly 76 percent) and Caucasian (80 percent). The majority of advisers who responded hold master's degrees (nearly 55 percent), while just under 30 percent have bachelor's degrees or less and the remainder (12.5 percent) have earned doctoral (Ph.D.) or other professional degrees (e.g. Ed.D., J.D.). The average number of years they have worked in international advising is 9.9, and they have been at their current campuses an average of 10.6 years.

In responding to an open-ended question in the study, respondents described a wide variety of paths that led them to the field of international advising. Many had some kind of prior exposure to international activities through their families, their college years, or their work experience. Typical responses included having parents who were immigrants or who hosted international students, studying abroad while in high school or college, majoring in a subject with an international component (foreign languages, anthropology, political science, etc.), and teaching English as a Second Language or being in the Peace Corps. A smaller segment of the group described how they "fell into" international advising by accident. Among this group were advisers who had been promoted from clerical or secretarial positions, were reassigned after a reorganization or sudden staff departure (e.g. resignation or death), or held another position in which international advising was just one piece of a larger set of responsibilities.

In our own experiences as well as those reported by others, serendipity seems to play a major role in becoming international advisers. One colleague attributed a career change to "divine providence," describing how his boss told him it was time to move on and "God intervened at the right time." The colleague said that experience taught him to be more future oriented and start thinking about the next career move before the boss suggests it. This haphazard type of career (non)planning may be a function of our age cohort (many senior international educators came of age in the 1960s and 1970s, a "hang loose" era when career counseling services did not exist on many campuses), our gender (women may be more open to changing careers than men), or simply our failure to plan ahead.

How Did You Get onto This Career Path in International Advising?

One of the great benefits of examining one's career past, present, and future in light of the career development research is that it allows one to make more strategic decisions at critical turning points. Some readers should already have a head start on identifying their key values, interests, talents, and skills if they've taken advantage of the array of career development services at their college or university. If you are not among them, your career services unit may offer the MBTI® and Strong Interest Inventory® Assessment to staff. Some international offices use these measures as team-building exercises so that staff can learn about one another in a nonthreatening environment. These types of assessment can draw out insights that you might not otherwise see; however, like many standardized measures, they tend to be most useful at discerning broad patterns and may not touch upon specific features that are more important to you individually.

In this regard, Rosser's study (forthcoming 2007) identifies certain characteristics and values that matter to international advisers. "What initially attracted you to international education, and specifically international student/scholar advising, as a career?" revealed patterns of job traits and values important to international advisers. The job traits tended to cluster around nonroutine activities and a diverse client base. Many advisers commented on the diversity of tasks and the need to keep learning new things. Some enjoy the intellectual puzzle of working out solutions to regulatory problems while others appreciate increasing their intercultural competence by interacting with students from a variety of countries. A number also said they enjoy working in higher education where learning is the mission.

With regard to shared values among international advisers, the most often cited was the notion of service, the desire to give back or help others. Many international advisers share this value because of prior international experiences in which they benefited from the generosity of others so now they are motivated to reciprocate; other advisers simply seem to have a passion for giving. The other key value reported by many is a desire for global understanding and peace. Older advisers attributed this to their "60s values," but both junior and senior advisers share the belief that they are personally contributing to greater understanding among the peoples of the world by doing the work they do.

If these descriptions don't sound like you, don't despair. As noted earlier, the Rosser study also found international advisers who came to their positions not by choice but because of institutional reorganization or reassignment. Some were thrust into their jobs when someone else resigned, retired, or died. Other respondents' comments reminded us that international education services at smaller institutions are often subsumed under other positions such as admissions officer, registrar, or counselor. For these administrators, advising international students and staying current on regulations may be more of a burden than a blessing; however, some people in this group noted that they really enjoy the international students and scholars and some even declared this their favorite part of their broader duties.

We recommend that new international advisers take the time to reflect on their career choice and how it suits various aspects of their personality, their values, their interests, and so on. If you find there are some critical aspects of the work that violate your core beliefs, it's probably not worth the stress of staying in the field. For example, the Iran hostage crisis of the late 1970s and the terrorist attacks on the World Trade Center in 1993 and 2001 prompted some advisers to leave their jobs as a matter of conscience because they disagreed with the increased reporting requirements imposed by the federal government. In more subtle ways, doing tasks you simply do not like may challenge the core motivations you have for being an international adviser. For example, some advisers chafe at the amount of time they spend on data entry in SEVIS; they aren't morally opposed to the reporting requirements but they very much resent the time spent on the computer when they would rather be engaging directly with students. This could drive some out of the profession, but for different reasons. We will revisit many of these issues in more depth in later chapters. We strongly recommend that readers take advantage of the follow-up activities at the end of each chapter so that they will be ready for those discussions.

Is There a Road Map for New Advisers?

We assume you have a job description for the position you now hold (if not, talk to your supervisor and get a copy now). There are probably elements in it that initially caught your eye and convinced you to apply. Now that you are in the position, it is a good idea to take a close look at that description and ask yourself a few questions. Was it written by someone who understands the special terminology (Designated School Official, for example)? Or was it written by someone who had only a vague idea of what an international adviser does? Does it need to be rewritten? This can be a constructive conversation to have with your supervisor in which you examine the mission statement and goals of your office, ponder the expectations of your various constituencies, and so on.

As a relatively new adviser, you probably are not in a position to dictate what you would like to have in your own job description, but you can do some homework that will help draw some boundaries and identify possible opportunities. There is an extended discussion of this under "Skill Sets" in Chapter 6.

Consider the example on the next page of a typical job description for an international student adviser position.

You will find that soliciting examples of job descriptions for people who are in similar jobs and/or who are at similar institutions is helpful. You always need to tailor your job description to your particular situation, but that doesn't mean you shouldn't tap other sources for interesting ideas. Your Human Resources department can probably give you some useful guidance regarding how your job description was developed. For example, they can tell you if the institution uses a structured classification system to create position descriptions. These types of systems identify key elements for all positions, e.g. scope of duties (who the position interacts with), level of responsibility (who the position reports to in the hierarchy), extent of decisionmaking (the amount of discretion the position is allowed to exercise), budgetary control (ranging from none to a lot), and so on. Or perhaps your campus has a highly individualized, even idiosyncratic, method for drafting job descriptions.

Compare the sample job description on the next page with yours. Does yours emphasize the duties that are the most important or the ones that take the most time? Does it focus only on the regulatory component of an international adviser position? Does your boss/unit/campus care about functions other than the regulatory component? Does your job description refer or relate to the vision, goals, and objectives of your office, unit, division, or campus? Is there a balance between the technical skills required and the "soft" skills that are so important to an international adviser position?

LE JOB DESCRIPTION FOR INTERNATIONAL STUDENT ADVISER

adviser will share responsibility for student advising (adjustment, cultural, and immigration) and programming activities in the Office of International Student Programs.

THE ADVISER WILL:

- Advise undergraduates and graduate students on adjustment issues, cross-cultural matters, and compliance with immigration regulations that apply for F-1 and J-1 students.
- Work as part of a team to design a comprehensive plan for social, cultural, and educational programs for the international community. This will occur in collaboration with various Student Affairs offices and other departments and student clubs.
- Work with students and the rest of a team to implement social, cultural, and educational programming for the university international community.
- Work in partnership with the counseling offices to provide appropriate counseling services for international students.
- Assist in planning and implementing a comprehensive orientation program for incoming students.
- Assist with SEVIS compliance.
- Provide support for university student groups. This includes help in planning student events as well as attending international events.

REQUIREMENTS INCLUDE:

- B.A./B.S., plus 2 years of relevant experience in an international student office
- Critical thinking skills
- Knowledge of U.S. immigration regulations as they pertain to F-1 and J-1 students
- Strong interpersonal, collaborative (oral and written) communication skills in a cross-cultural setting
- Understanding of U.S. higher education procedures and practices
- Strong time-management skills; ability to complete complex projects in a timely manner
- Experience with Word, database issues, and record keeping
- Candidates with experience in traveling or living in another country and/or knowledge of other languages in addition to English will be given preference.

SKILLS, KNOWLEDGE, AND ABILITIES:

- Ability to work in a cross-cultural environment
- Willingness to work with students for whom English is not the first language
- Excellent verbal and written English skills
- Ability to work in a complex, fast-paced environment
- Willingness to learn details and principles of immigration law
- Commitment to student adjustment and well-being
- Commitment to student confidentiality

A Variety of International Adviser Career Pathways

The pathways that advisers followed in the past will not bear much resemblance to the pathway you will create. You will find your own path, inventing the profession as you go—that's the adaptive and creative part. That may be part of what attracts you: the profession is not fully formed, there are few rigid "rules" or structures that govern the scope of your job, and there is a great deal of room for creativity.

Career paths of faculty are sometimes described in terms of being "cosmopolitan" or "local" (Gouldner 1957, 1958). This distinction may not fit international education administrators as well as it does professors, but there is some general relevance. According to Gouldner, both cosmopolitans and locals are loyal to their campus, but there are differences in how they conduct their day-to-day work. Cosmopolitans tend to have a high degree of commitment to their area of specialization and orient themselves toward outer reference groups. An example of this is a history professor who, in addition to teaching her classes, spends a great deal of time on research in her special area of fourteenth century Middle Eastern religious art and holds an office in a scholarly association for international historians. Locals, on the other hand, tend to focus on how their work supports the goals and mission of the campus and orient themselves to an inner reference group. This would be the professor who always serves on campus committees, provides crucial support to community organizations, and who may socialize at the faculty club, thus helping to provide the "glue" that holds the academic community together. This professor stays current on his/her field by reading journals but probably does not make presentations at the major scholarly conferences.

Following the approach of other career guides, we have mapped some stages that many international advisers go through, especially those who work full time in an international student or international education office. We recognize that many advisers work in very different environments so you will need to adapt the stages to make them fit your situation. Even if you fit the "typical" adviser profile, you should feel free to modify the stages, based on your own values, institutional context, and aspirations.

Note that we do not suggest how long any of the stages may last. If you are a fast learner by nature or your job demands that you master the skills quickly, you could be at the mature career stage in a very few years. Generalizing from "typical" career experiences, it can take ten or more years to reach the mature career stage. Remember that this isn't a race, it's your life.

Early Stage

During the early or beginning stage of their career, advisers typically concentrate on the following:

- Learning the basics of immigration regulations and procedures.
- Establishing and/or learning the basics of office operations, and campus protocols and procedures as needed.
- Building relationships with international student clubs.
- Developing a network of people on and off campus who can help with problems.
- Initiating professional involvement in member associations such as NAFSA (and NASPA, Student Affairs Administrators in Higher Education, especially if you do a lot of programming or want to improve your skills in this area); and attending local and regional meetings of associations and governmental agencies.
- Adapting to work in an intensely cross-cultural environment, starting the process of matching past cross-cultural training with day-to-day job demands.

This stage is office and campus focused. There is sometimes a jarring juxtaposition of hard technical skills (e.g. what does "D/S" really imply? Why can't we use "terminate" instead of "end program" in SEVIS?) and less tangible cultural skills (e.g. Why am I struggling so hard to communicate with the Korean club? Why do the Koreans and the Korean-Americans not want to combine their two clubs?).

Mid-Stage

In the mid-stage of their career, advisers often concentrate on:

- Deepening their understanding of immigration law. Some advisers at this stage decide to focus primarily on international students while others develop an interest in international scholar and employee immigration advising (i.e. J, H, and other employment-based visa categories.) This may change the individual's professional affiliate group somewhat.
- Reaching out to other units on campus to make sure office policies and protocols are aligned with other parts of the university.
- Mentoring newer staff in active involvement in student groups and community host programs, and building relationships with parts of the wider community interested in things international.
- Cultivating professional affiliations through active involvement in membership organizations such as NAFSA by acting as a mentor to people new to the field, attending meetings at which government officials speak, and presenting sessions at local and regional meetings.

- Increasing cross-cultural awareness of others on campus. This is usually done in subtle and quiet ways, mostly by good example and cooperative team work. It almost never happens in a formal didactic "let me teach you about how to relate to international students" manner.

This stage is often focused on issues outside basic international student concerns. For example, people in this stage often sit on university-wide committees dealing with crisis-response or town-and-gown concerns. The challenge at this stage is learning to operate comfortably outside the environs of the International Office where everyone shares the excitement of working with people from other countries and cultures. The Follow-Up Activities of Chapters 2 through 4 push you in this direction earlier than might happen without effort. It is, after all, one of the goals of this book, to help you develop your professional skills and abilities in a strategic manner that allows you to advance at your pace.

Management Stage

During this stage, senior advisers concentrate on the following:

- Teaching (rather than practicing) immigration principles.
- Reaching out to other international offices on a national level; comparing and fine-tuning office structures; and learning and then fine tuning management skills.
- Possibly moving into director position; mentoring other advisers; and advocating for resources to continue the work of the International Office.
- Possibly moving into leadership positions at either the regional or national levels of membership organizations; writing; consulting; taking a lead role in university advocacy; and acting as the contact person on immigration for your institution.
- Assessing the "internationalization" of the campus; and calling on long-term relationships to strengthen the appropriate global-awareness climate.

This stage is often focused on administration and management, sometimes to the exclusion of working directly with international students or scholars. The excitement comes from building a positive work environment that promotes the lofty goals of internationalism both on campus and in the wider world. People at this stage often have the chance to make a difference at a policy level, since they have a long history on campus and in the profession that lends credibility and a voice in the larger discussion.

Authors' Career Paths

We include the following biographies to demonstrate the routes by which we entered the field and navigated our careers. Remember, there is no "typical" pathway that international student advisers follow. Some routes may appear to be more straightforward than others, but all have their own internal logic, whether or not that logic is discernable. One caveat: we probably would have been more thoughtful in planning our career paths if we had read a book like this 20 years ago. So, we can only suggest at this point to follow the adage, "Do as I say, not as I do."

CAREER PATHS

I STARTED MY CAREER AS A MIDDLE SCHOOL TEACHER of English and history. Over the years, I combined graduate school and having children. Did I plan my graduate school carefully with an eye to a specific job? Of course not. I followed my completely impractical interests, which were art history, architectural history, and archaeology. I taught at the University of Colorado and at Colorado College for a few years.

At 40, I applied for a job in the international office because I had served as a teaching assistant on one of the university's summer programs in Italy (there are not many jobs where you get to go someplace wonderful, see great art, and help people understand underlying patterns and ideas). To my surprise and subsequent delight, I found myself on the "import" side of the international education equation. Over time I developed a keen interest in the regulatory side of the job, especially the regulations pertaining to scholars and faculty. I volunteered to help with NAFSA conferences, read the regulations, and generally immersed myself in tasks such as untangling regulatory language and creating materials to help with our everyday jobs. Gradually I became more interested in the advocacy part of regulatory work and served on a number of committees that dealt with these matters.

Without any merit on my part, I found myself working with some of the best international advisers in the business. They were patient, kind, and interested in helping me learn how to help international students and scholars, how to run an international office, and how to read the law. People have often asked me how I could be interested in things as seemingly diverse as art and the law. The answer is simple: it takes a passionate interest in art to spur one on to developing a critical eye and a critical mindset. In like manner, it takes a passionate interest in the human beings we work with to spur one on to developing a critical mindset about the law. The details of the law (no matter what kind of law) never seem interesting in themselves. But how the details of the law might help some interesting and worthy person accomplish his or her goal—now that's interesting!

Is this linear? Not at all. But it does have its own logic. You may find that your particular nonlinear path has its own elegant logic as well.

MARJORY GOODING

CAREER PATHS

I STARTED MY CAREER AS AN ESL TEACHER. Directly out of graduate school I taught in Japan, a country I first visited as a high school student (I attended a U.S. high school for military dependents in Okinawa, Japan's southernmost prefecture). I returned to the United States and spent several years teaching ESL in what proved to be not so much a career as a patchwork of part-time jobs: community adult education, refugee resettlement, intensive pre-university classes, and university classes.

Eventually, through a course instructor, I stumbled into an opportunity to be an international student adviser and I happily made the move. The international education office was small and understaffed, so I had the opportunity to develop my skills in a number of directions: immigration advising, programming, cross-cultural training—you name it, I did it. At the time, the institution was going through dire financial times and there were multiple reorganizations of campus units during my five years there. After one-too-many of these changes, I chose to leave. Unfortunately, it was in the midst of the post-Tiananmen Square Chinese student crisis of 1989–90, so I felt like I was deserting "my" students at their time of need.

Nonetheless, I moved on to my next position, which was in an integrated student services office where domestic and international students were all served as one group since they were represented nearly equally. I thought this was a position where I could happily spend the rest of my professional life managing a small staff while maintaining my technical and interpersonal international skills in visa regulations, programming, and services. Imagine my shock at being laid off five years later. No one gets laid off in education, do they?

While steering my career onto a new pathway at age 40+, I earned a Ph.D. with an emphasis far removed from international education and I survived by working a half-dozen temporary jobs, including a significant stint processing nonimmigrant employment visas in a Human Resources office. Subsequently I was recommended for my current position where international advising is a miniscule part of my work. This circuitous career path has been intellectually stimulating and rewarding, but it has been stressful and uncertain much too often. I learned rather late in life the importance of having a strategic map to guide my future, so readers should be encouraged to know that it is always possible to become more mindful of your career trajectory.

MELINDA WOOD

Looking Ahead

Once you delve more deeply into understanding yourself, how you got into international education, and the duties of the job you currently hold, you should have a good sense of whether this is a career path you will be happy to stay on for a while. If it looks promising, would you like to move up in the hierarchy and become an office director eventually? Would you like to explore some of the very interesting pathways that branch off of your current path, such as focusing on programming or becoming an expert in employment-based visa categories? Or maybe you recognized other factors you think are more important in shaping your future. Self-exploration often leads to unexpected findings. For example, maybe now you are comfortable acknowledging that where your children go to school is more important than where you go to work everyday, or that you are happy being limited to a particular geographic area because being near your parents or your favorite national park contributes more to your sense of self than your work does.

We are not suggesting that any one path is better, or more important, than another. We have provided some background information drawn from research on career development and the career of international student and scholar advising to encourage you to take the time to reflect on what matters to *you*. Once done, you should be much more prepared to make strategic decisions about the directions you want your career path to take you.

The following chapters cover some critical background information you will need, as well as a lot of practical guidance and suggestions for making the most of your career as an international adviser. Some of the information may seem irrelevant and unhelpful, but understanding it can give you an edge over other professionals in higher education who don't understand the complex context in which international education is set—in other words, the bigger picture.

FOLLOW-UP ACTIVITIES

1. Identify your key professional values and motivators. Use some of the career interest tools described in this chapter (e.g. Strong Interest Inventory®, Meyers-Briggs Type Inventory®). Ask yourself what you like most in your job: talking to students, solving problems, creating print materials, running cultural programs, and so on.
2. Have you considered how you would like your career to unfold in the future? How do you envision your career ten years from now? What would you like to be doing?
3. What would you like to be doing at the end of your career? Can you even imagine that?
4. Reread your job description. Arrange to have a conversation with your supervisor if you have questions or concerns after reading this chapter.
5. Do you have senior advisers in your office that are mentoring/training you, or who could mentor/train you?
6. Is there a local group of international advisers in your town or area that meets on a regular basis? Have you attended any of the meetings? If so, have you identified someone who can informally mentor you?
7. Do you have a current copy of the *NAFSA Adviser's Manual of Federal Regulations Affecting Foreign Students and Scholars*? If not, order one immediately!
8. Have you gone to NAFSA's Web site to see what resources (e.g. training, materials) they provide to members? Go to www.nafsa.org and put it in your Web browser "favorites/bookmarks" list right now.
9. Have you become a member of NAFSA: Association of International Educators?

Works Cited and Resources

Bloch, Deborah P. 2005. "Complexity, Chaos, and Nonlinear Dynamics: A New Perspective on Career Development Theory." *The Career Development Quarterly*, Vol. 53, p. 194–207.

Glazier, Lori, and Lori Kenschaft. 2002. "Welcome to America: The World War I Era and the Rise of International Education in the United States." *International Educator*, Vol. XI, No. 3, p. 5–11.

Gouldner, Alvin W. 1957. "Cosmopolitans and Locals: Toward an Analysis of Latent Social Roles." *Administrative Science Quarterly*, 2, p. 281–306.

Gouldner, Alvin W. 1958. "Cosmopolitans and Locals: Toward an Analysis of Latent Social Roles, Part II." *Administrative Science Quarterly*, 2, p. 444–480.

Holland, John L. 1973. *Making Vocational Choices: A Theory of Careers*. Englewood Cliffs, NJ: Prentice-Hall, Inc.

Kegan, Robert. 1982. *The Evolving Self: Problems and Process in Human Development*. Cambridge, MA: Harvard University Press.

Merkx, Gilbert W. 2003. "The Two Waves of Internationalization in U.S. Higher Education." *International Educator*, Vol. XII, No. 1, p. 6–12.

Mestenhauser, Josef. 1997. "Time and the International Educator." *International Educator*, Vol. VI, No. 4, p. 12–17.

Millett-Sorensen, Karin, and Skip Crownhart. 1985. "Foreign Student Advising as a Profession: The 1984 Survey." NAFSA *Field Service Working Paper* #4. Washington, DC: NAFSA: Association of International Educators.

Myers, Isabel B., and Katharine. C. Briggs. 1940. Myers-Briggs Type Indicator®. http://www.myersbriggs.org.

Rosser, Vicki J., Jill M. Hermsen, Ketevan Mamiseishvili, and Melinda S. Wood. Forthcoming January 2007. "The Impact of SEVIS on U.S. International Student and Scholar Advisors." *Higher Education: The International Journal of Higher Education and Planning*. Dordrecht: Springer Netherlands.

Strong, E. K., Jr., Jo-Ida Hansen, and David Campbell. 1927. Strong Interest Inventory® Assessment. http://www.cpp.com.

YOUR NOTES

A MAP OF YOUR PROFESSIONAL WORLD

CHAPTER 2

As a new international student adviser you may not be able to see beyond the edge of your desk right now, but you should know that your professional world is comprised of several large components, each with one or more distinct cultures. You will need to tend to all of them at some time or another in your career. There will even be times when the parts are in conflict with one another and you will have to be the cross-cultural ambassador engaging them in small scale diplomacy. Figure 2-1 shows the political map of what your career world may look like.

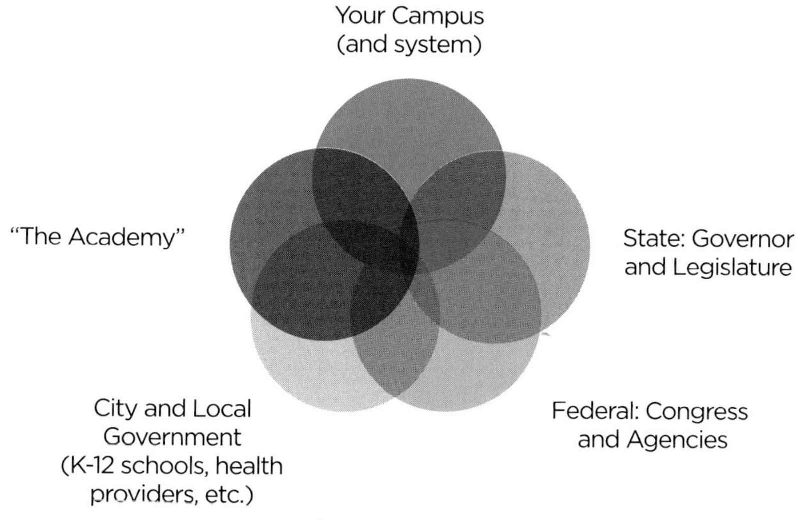

Figure 2-1. A Political Map of Your Career World

Students and scholars are not included in the diagram because they are the recipients or beneficiaries of the services that international advisers provide. The overlapping circles are the entities that influence your decisionmaking and shape the services you provide. The five components are described below with some guidance for understanding the unique culture(s) of each.

Who Benefits from Higher Education?

Each of the circles represents a different constituency, but they all grapple with the fundamental question of "who benefits from higher education?" Is it the individual who earns the degree and expects a successful career (and higher income) as a result? Clearly, this is a personal benefit. Or is it society that benefits from all the individuals who earn degrees and who, collectively, will pay more taxes on their increased income, will have better health because their jobs probably provide them with medical benefits, and statistically will be less likely to go to prison because they are contributing members of society (CollegeBoard 2005)?

The two perspectives of private good and public good are not mutually exclusive but tension between them is continually debated among legislators, faculty, and people in general. Let's take the case of Joe Bloggs, a 30-year-old retail sales clerk with a family of three. Joe just earned his B.A. and now qualifies for the management training program at the store where he works. Upon completing the program, his salary will go up about 20 percent. Part of his pay increase will allow him to buy a new car. This is a benefit to him and his family since he's currently driving a 1989 gas-guzzler with no airbags. At the same time, the new car will be safer for him and his children (potentially saving health care costs to his insurance company in case of an accident) and will get better gas mileage (which helps the environment), and he will have to pay county and state tax on the car (potentially helping to fill some potholes or other service need in his town). Thus, one can argue that there are many indirect benefits from Joe's college education that extend far beyond Joe and his family. This is one of the major issues that frame much of the debate between local, state, and federal governments regarding how higher education should be supported in the United States.

The debate is further complicated when international education comes into the mix. When international students earn a U.S. degree, how much of the benefit accrues to the students and perhaps their home countries? How do you think this factors into U.S. policy decisions? Hint: The revenue generated by international students in the U.S. is categorized as a service sector export by the federal government, suggesting that they consider international students to be taking knowledge out of the country. Yet it is equally appropriate to ask "to what extent do the receiving institutions and the United States, in general, benefit from them?" And certainly there is more than just money involved in this question. Do you think the balance between personal and public benefit shifts over time? Weighing these questions should help you articulate your views a bit more clearly by the time you finish this chapter and indeed, as you go through the rest of the book.

Higher Education in the United States—"The Academy"

According to Vartan Gregorian (2005, p. 30), the president of the Carnegie Corporation of New York:

> Today the American university is unquestionably the most democratic in the world. It is 'popular' in the best sense of the word, admitting and educating unprecedented numbers of men and women of every race and social class. Students from every imaginable background—and here I speak from personal experience—have found a place in this nation's incredible variety of colleges and universities. Today there are nearly 3,400 U.S. colleges and universities, including some 1,200 public and private two-year institutions. American colleges and universities enroll approximately 15 million students and grant around 2 million degrees each year. A $200 billion enterprise, higher education employs approximately 3 million people.

The next few pages will provide an overview that, we hope, is sufficiently detailed to give you the full flavor of the system that Gregorian describes and its unique culture but without overwhelming minutiae. We realize it may not be exciting reading for you right now, but it *will* be important in subsequent chapters so please stick with it.

Carnegie Classification of Institutions of Higher Education

American college and universities are often described by popularized categories such as Ivy League (institution age and status), Pac 10 (major athletic competitors), or media ranking (*US News and World Report*). Within higher education itself, the Carnegie classification system is considered the "industry standard" for sorting the multitude of postsecondary institutions in the United States. It is based primarily on institutional function and mission. The system was developed in the 1970s to help the Carnegie Commission on Higher Education conduct policy research. The fundamental categories have remained relatively stable over the years, but the 2005 update takes advantage of Web-based technology in creating a system that allows users to expand on the "basic" groupings by plugging in factors such as instructional programs, enrollment profiles, and size and setting to provide a more detailed analysis of subtypes. Many, if not most, campus administrators know which basic category their institution is in (though they may not be familiar with the most current terminology) and several peer institutions or competitors that share the same classification. The current major groupings are:

- Doctorate Granting Institutions (new scheme has three subsets instead of two, based on amount of research activity)
- Master's Colleges and Universities (three subsets instead of two, based on numbers of graduates earning degrees)
- Baccalaureate Colleges (three subsets based on proportion of students' majors: arts and sciences, diverse fields, and mixed 2-year and 4-year degree programs)

- Associate's Colleges (14 subsets based on urban/rural, small/medium/large, public/private, and other variables)
- Special Focus Institutions (nine subsets based on subject matter: faith, medical, health, engineering, technology, business, arts, law, and other)
- Tribal Colleges (institutions belonging to the American Indian Higher Education Consortium)

We could explain the classification system in more detail, but it would be much more instructive and useful for you to go to the Carnegie Foundation Web site, look up the descriptions, explore the categories, find your campus in the listings, and see what other campuses are in your category (www.carnegiefoundation.org/classification).

Culture of "The Academy"

From an organizational perspective, institutions of higher education have relatively flat hierarchies. But that doesn't mean they are simple organizations. Indeed, they are complex, often with a confusing array of semi-autonomous research entities, nonacademic outreach programs, affiliated but independent service units (e.g. bookstores, food services, housing), alumni and fund-raising organizations, and more. Some institutions have strong governing boards that are closely involved in the day-to-day operations of the campus while other institutions' boards maintain their distance and provide only broad oversight. Nonetheless, at the risk of gross oversimplification, one might contend that Figure 2-2 shows how university administrators tend to view their campuses.

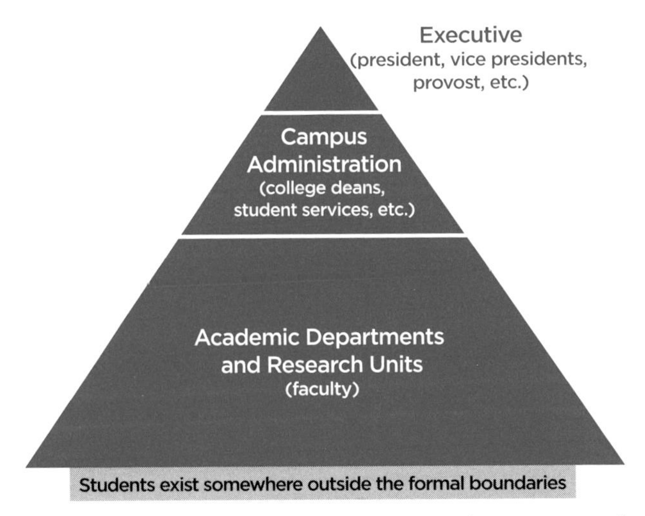

Figure 2-2. University Administrators' View of the Campus Culture

On the other hand, faculty view "the academy," that is, the academic enterprise of teaching and research as the core of the university while everything else is a loose collection of units that are there to support the academic function. There is a fundamental truth to this perspective—after all, can you imagine a college without professors? Faculty are intensively trained and socialized to be independent thinkers who push the limits of knowledge in rather narrowly focused academic disciplines. This background tends to prepare them to defend their discipline at all costs but not necessarily to consider the institutional perspective. Faculty value their academic freedom as essential to their work and rely on collegial peer pressure to make decisions rather than on bureaucratic policies and procedures. Administrators with institutional responsibilities that cut across academic units can become frustrated with faculty and complain that they are myopic and self-serving, but they simply have radically different views of their institutions. For illustration purposes, Figure 2-3 shows how faculty tend to see their campuses.

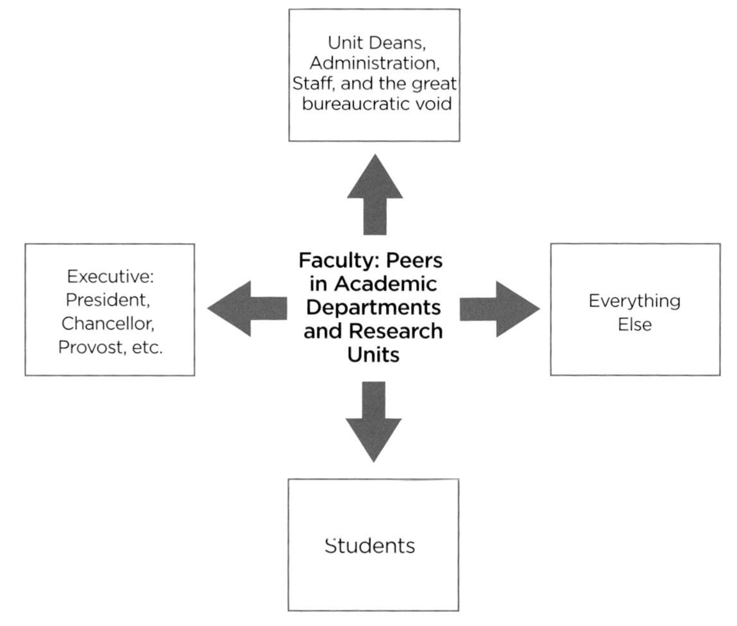

Figure 2-3. Faculty View of the Campus Culture

If you treat these differing organizational perspectives as cultural differences, instead of arguing with a professor about why you can or cannot do a particular thing for a student, you allow yourself to respond as you would in any other cross-cultural conflict—hopefully not by yelling at the person! For many of us with academic backgrounds in the liberal arts, the *terra firma* of Engineering may be at least as alien as Senegal or Tibet, maybe more so. Experience tells us that the English spoken by Australians is not exactly the same as English spoken by Americans; likewise, we should not assume that the language of faculty is quite the same as the language of administration.

To further complicate things, there are also subcultures within university administration. Student affairs/services units emphasize a holistic view of students and place a high value on creating developmental experiences that enhance the academic side of higher education. Many international student services offices are located in student affairs units, and international educators tend to share similar values and beliefs about what comprises a meaningful university experience for students. On the other hand, there are other administrative units—such as the office that manages contracts and grants or the facilities and maintenance office—that have virtually no contact with students. The subcultures of those units tend to be much more task-oriented and function largely outside the view of those who work with students. Thus you can rightly consider your campus to be a complex continent with numerous countries, each with its unique culture. As with any international sojourn, you should plan on visiting every country with an open mind and with a desire to get to know the inhabitants. Doing so will increase your appreciation of their cultures and will make your work more enjoyable.

SCENARIO | **The Angry Academic**

You have just started learning how to process employment visas for temporary researchers. Your supervisor is doing a good job of mentoring you in the technical aspects of what is required. One day when your supervisor is out sick, you agree to take the call when the chair of the geology department calls. He tells you there is an imminent eruption at a volcanic site he is studying, and he must get Dr. Izukawa here from Japan by the end of the week for six months of data analysis. You try to explain that you are new, your supervisor is out sick, and that to the best of your knowledge, these kinds of visas can take a few weeks to obtain. At the other end of the line, the chair loses his temper and explodes, calling you a ninny and shouting about mindless bureaucrats. He then slams down the phone, leaving you with a big headache.

Analysis

How can understanding the culture of "the academy" help you deal with this? How might you frame a culturally sensitive response if your supervisor will be out for the next two weeks? While there are numerous possibilities, the basic premise in developing a response is that you need to speak the faculty member's "language" to effectively communicate with him. What is salient to him is the science. He sees a short/small window of opportunity for this important (and to him, critical) scientific inquiry to happen. Nothing else matters because science is a religion to this faculty member. Helping him look for a temporary solution (e.g. Can Dr. Izukawa collect the data electronically and do the analysis from Japan? Would Dr. Izukawa want to come to campus as a "visitor for business" on the visa waiver program, stay only a short time, and receive only an honorarium?) has potential. The one thing that will definitely not help is lecturing the department chair on proper and timely planning. Sometimes even the best scientists are caught by surprise. By understanding his perspective, you can work toward a positive outcome and begin building credibility that will serve your future relationship with him well.

Once you have gotten through this situation, you should write down some notes and prepare questions to ask your supervisor when s/he recovers, such as:

- Have you dealt with this person before?
- Does s/he have a history of making last minute visa requests?
- Were you able to take care of him/her?
- Are there other faculty like him/her?
- What advice do you have for me in these kinds of situations?

How Money Works in Higher Education

Most institutions are funded by some mix of tuition, gifts and endowments, external grants, and sometimes state or church funds. You may be surprised about some of these sources and how they work.

Tuition Structures

The purpose of tuition is to offset the cost of educating students. Every institution or system has its own approach to setting tuition and fees. Some private institutions charge nearly the full cost to students and thus are very dependent on tuition to keep their doors open. Other private institutions rely on sources such as endowments or church support to keep tuition down. State systems generally subsidize the education of tax-paying residents of the state by charging them lower in-state tuition and charging much higher tuition to nonresidents. International students almost always pay out-of-state tuition at public institutions.

If you are at a public institution, you probably have seen for yourself one or more increases in tuition over the past few years. Because state legislatures have either cut appropriations for higher education or increased them by only very small amounts over the past several years, many institutions have been forced to raise tuition to balance their budgets and ensure continued access for qualified residents. According to the National Center for Public Policy and Higher Education, in 2003 "tuition and mandatory fee charges at four-year public institutions rose in every state. . .[and] community college tuition and mandatory fees rose in all but two states" (Trombley 2003). Depending on the size of the tuition increases on your campus, this may impact your ability to successfully recruit international students, especially those from less developed or economically stable countries.

A surprising fact that is not widely known is that regardless of the formula used, tuition alone *rarely* covers the full cost of educating an individual student. In fact, one definition of tuition is "Price [i.e., tuition] equals Cost minus Subsidy" where subsidy may take the form of state funding, endowments, or other funds (Lumina Foundation 2005). Thus, many institutions that count on international students to increase their revenue stream are probably increasing their costs at the same time. But you don't have to tell that to the people who only appreciate international students because they are "cash cows."

As long as international students are paying three to four times the tuition rate as in-state students at your institution, you have financial leverage. For instance, you can remind the dean about the total revenue that international students bring to the campus when you are advocating for more staffing in your office. Similarly, you will want to understand what exceptions are possible in the in-state tuition category. An example that touches international offices is that some state legislatures have determined that a person in H-4 status (the dependent of an international employee in H-1B status) is eligible for the in-state tuition rate. That can make a world of difference to an important visiting professor whose spouse or 19-year-old child would like to attend your university for a year. You might make a huge difference in that family's quality of life by ensuring that they are charged the resident rate to which they are entitled.

External Grants (Sometimes Called Contracts and Grants)

Institutions of higher education that have a significant research component have, of necessity, a strong relationship with various funding agencies. Some of these are private (example: The Bill and Melinda Gates Foundation); some are state (California has state funding for stem cell research), but most are federal.

> The end of World War II brought a profound change in the research and development efforts of the federal government. Increasingly, the U[nited] S[tates] turned to colleges and universities as a primary source for basic and fundamental research in science and technology. Initially, university research was sponsored by the Office of Naval Research (ONR), and the creation of the National Science Foundation (NSF) and the National Institutes of Health (NIH) provided a major impetus to the establishment of an infrastructure for the performance of basic research on college and university campuses throughout the nation. Growth in government funding grew steadily in the 50 years following WWII, and by 1997 federal awards for research and development in higher education institutions exceeded $15 billion. (National Association of College and University Business Officers (NACUBO) and the National Council of University Research Administrators, 2004)

Clearly, this is a significant sector of the U.S. economy and an even more significant portion of the higher education budget. It would be hard to overstate what this has meant to higher education. While most of this money goes to research-extensive and -intensive universities who are members of the Association of American Universities (AAU), some of it reaches smaller comprehensive or other types of institutions.

There are two channels through which federal funding is mostly likely to flow to campuses: competitive peer review and earmarking (Atwell 2005). The peer review competition is ostensibly a merit-based funding mechanism, but in fact it can be very difficult for smaller campuses to be awarded competitive grants. Earmarked funds are sometimes derisively described as "pork-barrel projects" and are officially opposed by higher education lobbying associations such as the AAU, but they can help campuses of any size to participate in federal support for higher education. Regardless of your institution's size and type, you can be pretty sure that someone on your campus cares a great deal about getting a share of this money.

Federally funded grants usually can be used for two types of institutional expenses. The first, direct costs, are those expenditures that colleges and universities incur in support of the institution's major, mission-related functions or activities. In most cases that activity is research (there are relatively few grants for teaching, outreach, and other activities). Many expenditures that accrue from conducting the research can be specifically attributed to the particular project or activity, hence the term direct costs.

The second type of expenses are those that are incurred for institutional activities not readily identifiable or directly assigned/connected with a high degree of accuracy to a major project or activity. These are called indirect costs. A simple way of understanding this is to realize that someone has to pay the light bill, put paper in the departmental copy machine, and take out the trash. These expenses that represent general operations are considered to be indirect costs.

There are closely regulated principles of cost reimbursement in federal contracts and grants. A question that pops up in administrative discussions on a regular basis is "Is that cost allowable (or allocable)?" An "allowable" item must benefit the account to which it is charged in proportion to the benefit. That might be very hard to determine, but there are grant administrators on campus whose job it is to do that calculation. The Dollars and Sense Case Study on page 102 in Chapter 6 provides an example where this knowledge will be an important part of the solution to a big problem for an international office.

Gifts: General Giving and Endowments

You have probably received any number of solicitations asking you to give generously to the colleges or universities you attended. This is among the most common means by which institutions raise additional funding. Many institutions have revamped their alumni offices, which in the past had mainly focused on newsletters and events to bring alumni back to campus, to become Development Offices, which are much more businesslike in leading organized "giving campaigns" to raise money and make new friends not only from alumni but also from non-alumni (an activity known as "friend raising"). Not surprisingly, most alumni donations tend to be relatively small and are not usually directed to specific projects.

Only recently have some institutions realized that they are missing the international sector of their alumni. If they have been particularly shortsighted, alumni/development offices may not have created sufficiently powerful databases to hold extra fields for international addresses or they may not want to spend the additional postage for international mailings. In such a case, you can be an invaluable resource for them and provide them with updates on students who are on practical training or students who have returned home and may be willing to start an alumni chapter overseas. Institutions that make efforts to keep in touch with their international alumni can have great success in raising funds as well as in recruiting and predeparture assistance for new students.

Many colleges and universities have special patrons who are vitally interested in some aspect of the institution and who donate large amounts of money in the form of an endowment. These donors often contribute for a specific purpose: they may be interested in astronomy so they fund a telescope purchase and the research that will utilize that instrument. They may be interested in medical research so they endow a professorial position (often called a "chair") that will be filled by someone who concentrates on appropriate research. Or they may be interested in the undergraduate experience and they donate money to cover the building and maintenance of a new residence hall. In 2005, more than 700 institutions reported endowments in excess of $1 million and the top 56 colleges each had endowments of $1 billion or more (NACUBO 2006), so endowments are clearly vital to the financial well-being of institutions.

Endowment money usually works a little differently than other gifts given to the university. An endowment is essentially seed money; it is to be held and invested in perpetuity. A portion of the annual return from the investment is used to support whatever designated purpose or purposes have been specified by the donor, if any. Most universities put all of their endowment funds into a consolidated pool and invest the pool in accordance with an investment strategy authorized by the Board of Trustees. The objectives are to maximize long-term total investment return, maintain and grow the purchasing power of the principal, and produce stable and predictable spending that is maximized and increases with inflation. This pooling is referred to as the total return concept.

An endowment has two parts. The first is a principal account, which is represented by a number of shares in the institution's consolidated endowment pool, much like a mutual fund. Over time, the market value of the endowment account will change with the market value of the consolidated pool. The endowment account's market value can be determined by reference to the number of shares it owns in the pool and the market value of a pool share.

The second part of an endowment is the associated spending account with its annual spending allocation. The annual spending allocation is determined by a university spending or "payout" formula approved by the governing board of the institution. The formula results in "spendable income" for distribution to each participant account based on shares owned at the beginning of the year. Generally speaking, most governing boards at institutions of higher education authorize a payout rate somewhere around 5 percent. So don't get too excited and jump up and down about that million dollar endowment you just got for an international center; the yield is only going to allow you to spend a tiny portion on the new facility.

City/County Context

We cannot begin to address the variety of types of city and county structures across the United States. Nonetheless, whether you work at an urban commuter campus in a major city, a sprawling residential campus in a college town, or at a small school in a rural community, there are bound to be "town and gown" issues that affect your work. For those not familiar with the origins of this term, "gown" refers to the robes that academics used to wear—you can see vestiges of them at some of the traditional British universities (and in Harry Potter movies). Some typical concerns that influence campus and community relations include:

- Does the campus have residence halls and any requirement for living on campus?
- Is there an active group of sororities and fraternities on or off campus?
- Is campus life sufficiently engaging for students, or do they go off campus for most of their social activities?
- How extensive are campus health care facilities, and for what kinds of medical care do students have to rely on community providers?
- Do students drink too much or engage in other problematic behaviors, either on or off campus?
- Is the campus a resource for community enrichment through events such as theater, concerts, and athletics that bring the community onto the campus?
- Is the campus the primary source of cultural and ethnic diversity in the community?
- Does the campus have married student housing, or do couples and families live off campus?
- Are spouses (both domestic and international) able to engage in meaningful activities?
- How many students have children enrolled in the local public schools?

These questions can apply to any type of institution in any size community. The answers of course will vary depending on your particular environment. Ideally, we all hope our institutions have a positive impact on their local community, but sometimes the problems outweigh the benefits. Some particular considerations for international students and scholars are:

- Where can they attend religious services?
- If they have children, how good are the local schools?
- Are there support systems for spouses?
- Where can they buy familiar foods and spices?
- Are there local issues about immigration or racial/ethnic diversity: illegal aliens, influxes of new immigrant groups, concerns about specific groups, anything that could spill over on to international students?

Once you have a pretty good understanding of your local "town and gown" dynamics, you should learn what your community government structure is. For many advisers who work in cities or towns where they have lived for years, this is usually easy. If you are new in your community, it can be baffling to figure out an unfamiliar system. Maybe you are used to a local government with a strong mayor and a weak city council, or a strong board of county commissioners with a nominal head. Whatever the case, it is useful to know who the players are and how they feel about your institution.

It also helps to know what the critical issues in the community are. What are the local industries and how are they doing? How is the housing market? What are the prevailing views about growth or development? What environmental issues are looming? What is the unemployment rate? All of these issues have an impact on your campus and you will want to understand those concerns.

State Context

Again, state governments are organized in so many ways that we cannot cover them all in depth; however, we can address the basics as they will impact your worklife as an international adviser. Every state has a governor and some type of legislative body. You need to know how the governor's office is organized, who is in the administration, and how your legislature is organized. Does it have one body (unicameral) or two (bicameral structure)? Who heads the legislature? Who represents the area where your campus is located?

More importantly, you need to know how state laws pertain to international students. Some of the most vexing problems you may face will be helping new students to open bank accounts, get driver's licenses, and sign leases without social security numbers and an easily recognizable form of identification such as a state ID card. These are often problems that really have to do with educating community members about legal alternatives, but you may find that there are state laws or local ordinances that create serious problems for international students and, in fact, need to be changed. When that happens you should be well prepared by having done your homework in advance.

One really important thing you need to know about your state government is the extent to which it funds higher education. Many people, even some who work in higher education, do not know the answer to this critical question. The proportion of funding dedicated to higher education gives you a general sense of its place in state government priorities. Allocation of state funds is a highly political process, influenced by an array of environmental factors such as past history, political context (e.g. relative influence of governors versus legislatures), economic conditions, and demographics such as changes in population or age groups (Layzell and Lyddon 1990). At the state level, higher education competes with several pressing issues, notably prisons, health care, and K-12 education. In response to increased demands in the latter three areas, nearly every state has reduced the proportion of funding it provides for higher education. On average, state support for higher education has fallen from more than 50 percent in the 1980s to just around 30 percent now, with some states contributing less than 10 percent (Lyall 2005). This means the other 70 to 90 percent has to come from other sources. The impact of this reduction is most obvious on public institutions, but it affects independent institutions as well, especially if you have a state financial aid scheme. There is evidence that in 2005 many state budgets began to show surpluses for the first time in many years so there is some hope that tuition increases can be slowed down and state support increased (Peterson 2006). But higher education will still have to compete with K-12 education and other state priorities that have also suffered through the lean years.

You will be much better able to discuss the role of international students and scholars to your campus' bottom line if you know what percentage of your institution's overall budget comes from direct state funding, what percentage comes from tuition, and if you are a public institution, what percentage is from in-state tuition versus out-of-state tuition. You can also find out if your campus receives scholarship funds from state sources, research funds from state or federal sources, or other income from gifts and endowments.

Federal Context

We cannot say it often enough: the field of international education in the United States changed dramatically in the wake of the September 11, 2001 terrorist attacks. At the national level, attitudes changed, priorities shifted, seemingly positive programs took on what were seen by some as having sinister overtones, racial profiling became an acceptable tool to some, and the legal matrix in which we operate became decidedly more cautious. The unanticipated outcomes from these kinds of world-changing events continue to change the context in which international education operates.

The relationship international advisers have with the Department of Homeland Security and the Department of State since September 11 has become more structured and more visible. Understanding some basic organizational principles of these bureaucracies makes the day-to-day operations in an international office run more smoothly. It also lays the foundation for becoming an effective advocate for international students and scholars. If you want to have any voice in changing laws or regulations, you have to know the players and the agencies in which they operate.

Understanding the Basic Structures

The statutes that govern immigration and visa acquisition are *federal* laws, passed as bills by the U.S. Congress and signed into law by the president. Federal agencies charged with administering and enforcing these laws also create federal law in the form of federal regulations. The states generally have no part in the enforcement of immigration laws, but you may hear public debate taking place on that topic. The *NAFSA Adviser's Manual* provides an excellent introduction to the hierarchy of authority in federal law and regulation. Read it. You'll be surprised at how much better prepared you will be for discussions on immigration topics.

Immigration Law

Most federal laws are an accretion of ideas and attitudes of U.S. lawmakers over a period of many years. Immigration law is no exception. As a nation of immigrants, the United States in its early years had no laws that addressed who could enter or what circumstances would limit entry. Beginning in the late nineteenth century and on through the middle of the twentieth century, laws were enacted that excluded specific groups deemed at the time to be "undesirable." For example, in 1882 laws excluded "idiots, lunatics, and convicts;" that same year, the Chinese Exclusion Act was passed and remained on the books until 1943 (Kurzban 2004-2005). These laws formed a patchwork of different statutes until 1952, when the Immigration and Nationality Act (INA) was drafted. Since then, each new and/or different provision of immigration law adopted by Congress is blended into the INA, giving us a structure into which such diverse topics as asylum, international student regulations, or international employment can be placed.

Immigration Regulations

That important topics, like provision for international students to come to the United States, are covered in only a *very* general way in the INA is a revelation to some. The section on F-1 students in the INA is only a couple of paragraphs. How could that be? International advisers spend so much time sorting through the legal provisions! This happens because the statute is the general directive from Congress. The details are left to the federal agencies (in this case, the Department of Homeland Security) charged with writing the regulations.

The F-1 regulations, in turn, are relatively brief compared with others—just a few pages. If regulatory matters consume so much time and energy, shouldn't the regulations be extensive? The answer is that the application of law and regulation is an art, not a science. International students and scholars present advisers with the full spectrum of their fascinating and complex lives so it is up to the adviser to make that complexity fit into what are ostensibly "simple" regulations in a sensible, accurate, consistent, and humane way.

Federal Agencies

Department of Homeland Security (DHS) and its constituent parts are responsible for promulgating and enforcing immigration regulations. The constituent parts are:

- U.S. Customs and Border Patrol (CPB)—responsible (among other things) for "inspecting" internationals coming to the United States for many purposes.
- U.S. Immigration and Customs Enforcement (ICE)—responsible for all immigration enforcement activity, including SEVIS.
- U.S. Citizenship and Immigration Services (CIS)—responsible for adjudicating applications for immigration benefits such as change of status or permanent residency.

Department of State (DOS) is responsible for formal nation-to-nation relationships between the United States and other countries. It is a huge organization with vast power and scope—a brief surf through their Web site will give you some idea of just how vast. There are a few parts of DOS that international advisers must understand to do their jobs.

The United States has diplomatic relations with most, but not all, countries in the world. The U.S. "presence" in these countries is housed in the U.S. embassy, and the U.S. delegation is headed by the U.S. ambassador to the particular country. The ambassador and the embassy are responsible for many functions such as trade relations, cultural affairs, and consular affairs, among others. Each embassy will have a *consulate* where visa matters are attended to. Depending on the size of the host country and/or the complexity of the relationship, there may or may not be additional consulates located in other cities or regions of the host country. An individual who seeks a U.S. visa must apply to the U.S. consulate that has jurisdiction over the area in which he/she lives. Of particular interest to international advisers are the Web sites of the various U.S. consulates. Detailed information on each is available at www.travel.state.gov.

The Bureau of Consular Affairs is the part of the U.S. Department of State that deals with visa acquisition. Its main office (the Visa Office) is in Washington, DC. This is where policy directives are formulated and communicated to consulates all over the world. Communication from the Visa Office to the consulates/posts takes the form of cables. These are, of course, distributed electronically rather than in "cable" form, but the formal name of this mode of communication persists.

The Exchange Visitor Program (EVP) is part of the DOS Bureau of Educational and Cultural Affairs. It administers the J visa, which is widely used by colleges and universities for a variety of exchange purposes. The Bureau authorizes institutions to issue the Form DS-2019, allowing individuals to obtain a J visa and come to the United States.

Your Campus

Having outlined some of the relationships, issues, and cultural contexts that affect higher education in general and local, state, and federal politics, we can now get back to the most important piece of the puzzle—YOUR campus. Again, because every campus is distinctive, with its own culture, subcultures, politics, and concerns, we can only guide you through some questions that will help you learn more about your institutional context and culture and how it interacts with the other entities we have described.

By now you should know your Carnegie Classification type. You know if your institution is public or private. One factor that may contribute to the culture of your campus is whether you are part of a system of campuses (e.g. State University of New York or University of California) or a freestanding campus. Is your institution relatively new, or does it have a lengthy history and longstanding traditions? If you are at a primarily teaching institution, what are some of the key values about learning and faculty/student interactions?

If you are at a research university, federal funding will have a major impact on how your institution operates. There will be many more faculty and staff who deal with federal regulatory matters and perhaps deal with international scholars and faculty who will need your assistance in getting a visa. You should find out more about any affiliated but quasi-independent research units or institutes that have a relationship with your campus. Many universities have collaborative relationships with such organizations; however, few people understand what the relationship is and how it works. Some interesting examples from our own work experiences include: the Keck Telescope Observatory in Hawaii, which is administered under the auspices of the University of California-Berkeley; the Gemini Telescope in Hawaii, which is operated by the Jet Propulsion Laboratory in conjunction with the California Institute of Technology; and the National Oceanic and Atmospheric Administration labs, which conduct joint research with the University of Colorado in Boulder. There are many more examples that you can probably find through your own investigations.

Why Does Any of This Matter to You?

You may spend most of your time sitting at a desk in an office, but your professional world is vast. You need to explore that world just as thoroughly as if you were on an actual journey. We strongly encourage you to physically get out and examine your campus and community through the investigative lens of an international educator. You may not be able to physically go to all the state and national sources we have described in this chapter but you can certainly tour them virtually from your desk. This exploration can and should be at least a tiny bit fun, but more importantly, it lays the foundation that you need to be an effective international adviser and university administrator.

FOLLOW-UP ACTIVITIES

1. Go to the Carnegie Web site and examine the descriptions of the various classifications. Find your institution and some of its peers. www.carnegiefoundation.org/classification/index.asp
2. Investigate your campus history: Who are the various buildings and streets named for? What are the famous landmarks and why are they famous? What significance do gardens and landscaping have? What are the major campus events and why are they important?
3. Find out who runs the Development or Alumni Office on your campus. Conduct an "informational interview" to learn how your institution's giving and endowment program is structured or if it exists. Learn the difference between restricted and unrestricted monies. Who knows? Your Development Office may be interested in partnering with you to establish an international chapter of the Alumni Association
4. See if you can find out the answers to the following funding questions:
   - What percentage of your institution's overall budget comes directly from state funding?
   - What percentage of your institution's overall budget comes from tuition? If you are at a public institution, what percentage of your institution's overall budget comes from in-state tuition? Out-of-state tuition?
   - What percentage of your institution's overall budget comes from federal research funding?
   - What percentage of your institution's overall budget comes from state research funding?
   - What percentage of your institution's overall budget comes from endowment payout?
   - Has a change in political party made a difference in state funding for higher education in your state?
5. If you haven't done it already, read Chapter 2 of the *NAFSA Advisers' Manual*. Go to the Web site and check out the links to original sources.
6. Explore the DHS and DOS Web sites at www.dhs.gov and www.state.gov . Put these and the SEVIS Web site into your "favorites/bookmarks" list.
7. City/County: Get the names and contact information for your mayor and city council members. Put that information in a handy place where you can always find it.
8. City/County: Read your local newspaper(s) daily.
9. State: Get the name(s) and contact information for the legislator(s) who represent the district where your campus is located.
10. Federal: Get the name(s) and contact information for your two U.S. senators and congressional representative for the district where your campus is located.

Works Cited and Resources

Atwell, Robert H. 2005. "The Pork Barrel Revisited." *The Presidency*, Vol. 8, No. 1.

Carnegie Foundation for the Advancement of Teaching. Information retrieved April 2006. www.carnegiefoundation.gov.

CollegeBoard. 2005. *Education Pays Update* 2005. Trends in Higher Education Series, www.collegeboard.com/trends (accessed February 2006).

Gregorian, Vartan. 2005. "Leading Today's Colleges and Universities: Challenges and Opportunities." *The Presidency*,Vol. 8, No. 2, p. 29–33.

Kurzban, Ira J. 2004-2005. *Kurzban's Immigration Law Sourcebook*, Ninth Edition. American Immigration Law Foundation.

Layzell, Daniel T. and Lyddon, Jan W. 1990. *Budgeting for Higher Education at the State Level: Enigma, Paradox, and Ritual*. Washington, DC: The George Washington University in cooperation with the Association for the Study of Higher Education.

Lumina Foundation for Education. 2005. "Dreams Detoured." *Lumina Foundation Focus*, Fall 2005. www.luminafoundation.org (accessed February 2006).

Lyall, K. April 2005. "A Call for the Miracle Model." *Carnegie Perspectives*. www.carnegiefoundation.org/perspectives/perspectives2005.April.htm

National Association of College and University Business Officers (NACUBO). January 2006. *National Endowment Survey Results*. www.nacubo.org

National Association of College and University Business Officers (NACUBO), and the National Council of University Research Administrators (NCURA). December 2004. *A Guide to Managing Federal Grants for Colleges and Universities*.

Peterson, K. February 22, 2006. "State Surpluses a Boon to Education." *Stateline.org: Where Policy and Politics News Click*. The Pew Research Center. Retrieved from www.stateline.org

Trombley, W. Winter 2003. *The Rising Price of Higher Education. College Affordability in Jeopardy: A Special Supplement to National Crosstalk*. The National Center for Public Policy and Higher Education.

YOUR NOTES

BUILDING YOUR NETWORK OF ALLIES

CHAPTER 3

As noted earlier, many international advisers share a belief in the concept of service. In general, service is a highly people-oriented activity, one that international advisers often relish and demonstrate their commitment to by developing a positive environment for international students and scholars. This does not mean you have to be gregarious and extroverted all the time, but you do need to be (and *should* be) willing to go out and talk to other people. If you tend to prefer the paperwork aspect of the job over human interaction, you might find this chapter's networking tasks daunting. We highly recommend that you take this in small increments. Don't plan on having a fully formed network all at once—it takes time to nurture relationships.

You were introduced in Chapter 2 to the interrelated constituencies that comprise the bigger picture of higher education in the United States. Now you need to identify individuals in each of the groups with whom you can find common ground. Just as when you move to a new country, once you have the basic lay of the land, you will want to know where you should go to meet people with similar interests.

Not surprisingly, there are many people both on campus and in the community who rarely, if ever, encounter international students or scholars. Unfortunately, their occasional interactions do not necessarily reinforce the "to know them is to love them" cliché. Some of these intercultural novices find international students to be demanding, rude, or just plain strange. To counter these views, you should seize every possible opportunity to network with faculty and staff and let them know what you do. Get on the campus recycling committee. Visit the health center. Attend athletic events. Chances are you will also find people who studied abroad during their college years, had a Fulbright grant to do research overseas, perhaps have a spouse from another country, or are immigrants themselves (who perhaps first came here as international students). At the very least you might learn who went to France for their honeymoon or who camped in Mexico for six months after the dot-com bust. Someone might have been a "military brat" who lived overseas and speaks two foreign languages. Maybe there is a dean who loves opera and goes to Italy every year. Perhaps someone belongs to a church that sponsors an international mission or hosts a choir that visits your town.

Some of these people may not be immediate allies for international students, but with care and attention they can be cultivated. How do you go about that? First, you need to learn what is important to your potential allies. What aspects of campus life or academics matter to them? Are they concerned about the academic preparation of minority students? Underage drinking on campus? Landscaping that has been neglected? Surely you can find some connection and, ideally, a way in which international students may become part of a solution for their concerns. How about a program where international students trade math tutoring for English conversation? Creating an international peace garden by international students in horticulture? Developing these alliances can be one of the most creative aspects of what we do.

Knowledge and exposure to people from other countries is equally lacking at the state and national level, even in the most diverse states with high rates of in-migration. Some people who work in government agencies or hold elective offices may already have a track record as allies for international education while others may need nurturing to see the benefits of international education. Some individuals, unfortunately, may be a hindrance without even realizing it. One anecdote (or urban legend) heard among international educators is that some members of the U.S. Congress interact with non-U.S.-born citizens only when they are being driven around the nation's capital by immigrant taxi drivers. This sounds pretty strange to devoted international educators, but keep in mind that statistics indicate that as many as 80 percent of Americans have never had a passport (data are hard to find; best estimates reported in the popular press claim that 20–22 percent of U.S. citizens hold passports).[1] Creating a "culture" of engagement and interest in international education at all of the levels described in Chapter 2 *is* part of our jobs.

The information in this chapter is only a starting point! These examples are drawn from our own experiences and knowledge of U.S. higher education in general. You need to identify the specific offices and individuals in your own environment that match or correlate with what we've provided. Each unit or office we discuss will have unique members, culture, and history in your context or location that may radically alter the suggestions we list below.

[1] An Internet search found these figures cited in articles from the San Francisco Chronicle, YaleGlobal Online (from Yale University), About, Inc. (a part of the New York Times Company), and numerous travel sites. None of these sources gave references. Frank Moss, Deputy Assistant Secretary for Consular Affairs, testified to the U.S. House of Representatives Homeland Security Committee Subcommittee on Economic Security, Infrastructure Protection, and Cybersecurity on June 22, 2005 that 8.8 million passports were issued in Fiscal Year 2004; it is not possible for us to extrapolate a total number of passport holders from this figure.

Campus Allies

Student Affairs

Most international offices are located in a larger Student Affairs unit. You might think at first glance that the Offices of Residence Life, the Registrar, or the Bursar (entities that usually come under Student Affairs) are unlikely partners to an International Office. Not so. Since all international students must engage each of these functions, you will find that you have essential business operations that overlap with these offices. Understanding their functions will guide you. For example, the Registrar is usually the official keeper of student academic records and is charged with reporting this data to the federal government (international educators aren't the only ones required to report student information). This is done primarily through the Integrated Postsecondary Education Data System (IPEDS). According to the National Center for Education Statistics, "IPEDS, established as the core postsecondary education data collection program for NCES, is a system of surveys designed to collect data from all primary providers of postsecondary education. IPEDS is a single, comprehensive system designed to encompass all institutions and educational organizations whose primary purpose is to provide postsecondary education" (The National Center for Education Statistics 2006).

This explains why the data provided for the *Open Doors* (Institute of International Education 2005) report should come from the Registrar. It is tempting to pull that data from your office's stand-alone data system, but that ignores an essential rule of the university—someone is already designated as the official source for academic information about students. If you work in partnership with the Registrar, not only will your data be more accurate, but you will be working in concert with the overall structures of the University. A partnership begins....

Within Student Affairs, you should be able to find a number of partners in programming. Residence Life or Housing Offices are always looking for new program ideas. If you can work with them on creating cross-cultural activities that go toward happier living arrangements among U.S. and international students, you will have strengthened a relationship that is sometimes needlessly problematic. Another example is the Women's Center. If you spend a little time with the director of the Women's Center, you may find that she has excellent ideas for joint programs. What a great service you could provide if you partnered in offering a self-defense session tailored particularly to the international women on campus. Similarly, you may find a great programming partner in the Counseling Center. Having a hard time making an international student support group work? You may need some help from the pros. Conversely, if the counselors have no particular interest or expertise in cross-cultural adjustment issues, inviting them to attend your "adjusting-to-life-in-the-U.S." session during orientation might spark their interest. At the end of the day, you definitely want to know the person you will be working with when an international student runs into significant psychological trouble.

In general, Student Affairs staff members share a zeal for helping students to get the most out of their college or university experience, similar to the passion described by many international advisers (Rosser et al. forthcoming 2007). Thus they are likely allies though some individuals may be novices with the international component. This is relatively easy to fix with knowledge and positive experience, which you can certainly provide.

Academic Affairs

As the name indicates, this part of any campus concerns itself with the academic business of the institution. In a nutshell, Academic Affairs is responsible for delivering degree programs. Some of its functions typically include oversight of curriculum and degree requirements, tenure and promotion decisions for faculty, program reviews of academic departments, and accreditation. Some campuses use the title Provost for the executive head of Academic Affairs; other campuses have a Vice President or Vice Chancellor in this role. Some institutions have moved to a more corporate model and call this person the Chief Academic Officer. If you are not sure of the nomenclature, ask your boss for help. The people at the top of the Academic Affairs pyramid tend to have little contact with students outside of commencement ceremonies or other formal occasions, and they may not even have a lot of routine contact with individual faculty members. Depending on the size and organization of your campus, you may be among those with little reason to interact with these people; however, they should not be disregarded as allies.

Deans and directors are usually at the next level down the academic hierarchy. These are the academic leaders who oversee clusters of departments and other types of academic units such as the honors program. And it goes without saying, departments are comprised of faculty. These are the academic people who are most likely to be your allies. Get to know faculty members who are former international students themselves, Fulbright alumni, and study abroad group leaders. Do not limit your search for allies to departments like foreign languages and anthropology. Many faculty members in technical or scientific fields are often deeply interested in international students because of research projects in other parts of the world. Similarly, research faculty understand that a high percentage of their students and post-doctoral scholars are international.

Government Relations Office

Find out who on your campus deals with government relations. Ask your boss if s/he already has a working relationship with that person. Regardless of whether the answer is yes or no, ask your boss to set up a get-acquainted meeting that includes you. Consider taking that person to lunch (with your boss's permission) or conduct an informational interview to find out what he/she does for your campus: is the focus mostly on state or federal relations, or both? What other levels of government does the office cover? What other kinds of work is the office responsible for? For instance, government relations may be under the General Counsel's office (see below), in which case they may spend much more time on litigation and preventing litigation than on government relations.

As you will see in the next chapter, your institution's official comments on governmental matters will probably be orchestrated through this person's office. Clearly, this is someone to cultivate as an ally; having the government relations person trust your knowledge of immigration law as it pertains to international student and scholar issues will be critical to building that relationship.

Office of General Counsel

Not all colleges or universitites have an office dedicated to the legal matters of the institution, but all will have at least an attorney on retainer to deal with institutional legal needs.This person or office has as its charge representation of the institution in legal matters. In rare cases, an international scholar office may report through the Office of General Counsel. Ask your supervisor how this is arranged on your campus. If possible and appropriate, conduct an informational interview with someone in this office. As with many other campus functions, you'll want this person to know you and trust your judgment if there is ever a problematic case. You definitely want to consult with this office in the event that officials from the Department of Homeland Security or other law enforcement agencies make a visit to your campus.

University Relations/Public Relations/Media Relations

This office may go by any number of names. Get to know the people who release/distribute institutional materials that carry news and features about the campus—Web sites, publications, or mass e-mail. Are these the same people who feed campus press releases to local community media? They often need story ideas. Give them notice of your colorful events and other stories so that they can promote your office and make the necessary community contacts for further coverage. You have access to some of the best local angles and human interest stories that can make a national or international story real to your community. You may be surprised how interested people are.

Human Resources Office

Depending on the scope of your job description, you will probably need to have allies in your Human Resources (HR) office. Because international students are allowed to work on campus and most institutions have a variety of student employment classifications, you should become familiar with the full spectrum of employment opportunities. On some campuses, you will find a vexing array of separate offices that oversee various types of on-campus jobs for students (e.g. work-study, hourly, co-op), but in some institutions HR handles all categories of employees, including student workers.

If your job description includes responsibility for J-1 exchange visitors, it is fairly safe to assume that visiting faculty and researchers will interact with the HR office, so you would be well served in getting to know the key staff members. If your duties include employment-based visas, then you definitely need to have a good working relationship with the HR staff. Table 3-1 may be helpful in describing some of the most common functions within Human Resources and how their actions might affect your office.

Table 3-1. Human Resources and the International Office

HR UNIT	HR FUNCTION	RELATIONSHIP TO INTERNATIONAL OFFICE
BENEFITS	Negotiates terms of health insurance packages, administers sign-up	If the Benefits office doesn't know that the J regulations require special care, this might get left out.
EMPLOYMENT	Helps hiring departments find qualified candidates, conducts searches, etc.	If the Employment office doesn't know that green card applications require special recruitment, the green card application might fail.
COMPENSATION	Creates job families, determines salary levels, determines placement of a particular job in a particular job family.	If the Compensation unit isn't aware of the prevailing wage requirements for research positions, you may have trouble filing H petitions for your university's postdocs.
EMPLOYEE RELATIONS (ER)	Help supervisors conduct fair disciplinary procedures, work with Payroll staff to take people off the payroll when their employment authorization expires.	If ER doesn't understand that employment authorization is date-specific for some internationals, they may ignore important dates, resulting in legal problems for the international and for the institution.

The Payroll Office is not included in this chart because it sometimes resides in another campus unit such as Business and Finance. Regardless of where it sits, you will want a good working relationship with the payroll people. Just as we are required to comply with federal regulations regarding immigration status (housed in the Department of Homeland Security (DHS)), they are required to comply with federal regulations regarding taxation (the Internal Revenue Service (IRS) is housed in the Department of the Treasury). Unfortunately, the two federal agencies use the same words in their regulations, but they define them in very different ways. For example, the IRS uses the term "resident alien" to describe a particular type of individual for tax purposes, but DHS uses it to describe a completely different type of person for immigration purposes. Discussions of who is and who is not a "resident" according to tax versus immigration regulations can be both hopelessly frustrating and mind-bogglingly entertaining. Throw in a few tax treaty questions and it will drive sane people over the edge. Getting to know the Payroll staff and talking about this in advance of a disagreement over an individual case is a really good idea. Building bridges is key to clear communication.

We are *not* suggesting that you become an expert in taxation, even though the Payroll Office may come to you and say, "It's international stuff—you're *supposed* to do this kind of thing!" No, you aren't. You can help them to find tax publications and resources, you can commiserate over the bureaucratic language, and you can build an alliance that will serve you both well. Because there is no regulatory niche in the tax code for international advisers (remember that this niche does exist in immigration law), tax advising is *not* a job responsibility of most international advisers.

Campus Security

Generally speaking, international students and scholars have few encounters with the campus security. But the occasional problem does arise. Build a relationship with the officers in advance. Think about inviting an officer to come to your new student orientation to talk about how students can enhance their safety on campus (but don't scare them needlessly, please). While the students themselves may be relatively confident about their safety, overseas media impressions of the United States can be especially frightening for parents. This session can serve three purposes: 1) correct any misconceptions the students may have; 2) give the students something to tell their worried parents on the phone; and 3) set the stage for a good partnership with Campus Security.

Campus Crisis Management Team

What constitutes a crisis on/for your campus? We made reference earlier, in Chapter 1, to a number of large scale crises that have occurred in international education. However, your campus is more likely to be affected by a disaster that does not have an inherently international dimension—except for the international students and scholars who are caught up in it. Campuses in California have experienced severe earthquakes, and institutions along the Gulf Coast have suffered catastrophic hurricanes and flooding. Even relatively localized events such as fires or tornadoes have affected campuses across the country. Then there are crises of the human type. Some of these have direct effects on large numbers of people (campus snipers, bomb threats, etc.) while others may involve few people directly but many indirectly (murders, suicides, accidents).

To be prepared for any and all of these situations, the first thing to do is obtain a copy of your campus emergency plan (every campus has one even though people may not know about it) and read it carefully. Most institutions have strict protocols regarding who does what in an emergency. Virtually every campus in the country has reviewed and upgraded its emergency response policies and procedures since September 11, 2001. You need to know where you fit into that plan and what your institution expects of you as a professional staff member. You also need to meet with your boss to learn about your office's crisis plan for dealing with events that affect international students and scholars. An excellent example of crisis management from the entire international education community was the coordinated response to Hurricane Katrina in 2005. While the advisers at the affected institutions helped to evacuate their campuses, other advisers were working with DHS to develop expedited processes for transferring the displaced students to other institutions and others were helping to get them admitted to those new institutions without full records.

Community Allies

You know that your institution is just one part of a larger community. You may live in that community and know it well. Alternatively, you may live at a distance and not know much about the culture or politics of the area surrounding your institution. Whatever your particular set of circumstances, you will find that the neighboring community is a great potential resource for your office. As with all possible boons, there are some cautions.

Friendship Groups

Some novice international advisers have made the mistake of overlooking the importance of local host family or friendship groups. They may think, "They're just a bunch of old people," or "They will try to make the students go to church." Local host or friendship groups can be invaluable allies when you take the time to develop a mutually beneficial and trusting relationship with them. You will probably find people who have had international adventures beyond your imagination (e.g. Peace Corps volunteers from the 1960s who lived in countries like Iran and Afghanistan, where few Americans would be inclined to travel at the moment) and people who have their own networks in the community (and who are far more influential than most of us are likely to ever be).

These groups have the potential of providing a much-needed respite for international students, especially during holiday breaks when domestic students tend to disappear from campus. Having a chance to attend a "real" American Thanksgiving dinner is intriguing to many international students. The inviting family certainly needs to understand that religious or political proselytizing is not an acceptable part of the event. If you have a good working relationship with the leaders of the host family program, you can work with them to develop a training program so that host families understand the boundaries of this kind of hospitality.

We cannot stress enough that your commitment to advising international students and the community people who share that commitment must adhere to NAFSA's Code of Ethics (printed in Appendix B of this book) when it comes to religious practice and proselytizing. It was noted in the study conducted by Rosser et al. (forthcoming 2007) that a good number of international advisers have an almost religious fervor for the importance of their work, and they bring a missionary zeal to fulfilling their broader ideals of increasing global understanding and peace. However, this deeply held commitment should not be confused with or overwhelmed by actual religious practice. NAFSA's Code of Ethics strictly prohibits the use of one's position as a means of religious proselytizing or attempting to convert students to a particular faith. There are, in fact, advisers who openly bring their religious beliefs and community into their work and integrate them in subtle or not-so-subtle ways that push the limits of ethical behavior.

Friendship or host groups can also be your allies when you need help influencing others. They are almost always great advocates for greater campus resources for international students, they can write to state legislators and city council members, and write letters to local newspapers. But you need to nurture this relationship and demonstrate that you can be counted on for help.

Home Country Cultural and/or Religious Groups

A local immigrant group, community mosque, or temple may be a touchstone for an international student or scholar. The caution, of course, is that the welcoming organization must respect the boundaries that the international student sets. Some international students find that they share little with an immigrant group from the same country if there are vast differences in class, religion, or home region. They may not be interested in second or third generation immigrants who look like them and eat the same food but do not speak the language. On the other hand, in times of natural disasters or political crises, these groups can be important lifelines that connect international students to their families and home country. Thus, these types of groups can be strong allies for you in the community.

While you cannot control everything that students or scholars encounter in the broader community, you should know something about the community organizations that invite international student participation. You are not a parent to the students, but you certainly should know something about those who are interested in them.

Local Media

When was the last time you read a heartwarming story that had something to do with international education? We couldn't remember either (okay, we exaggerate, but only slightly). It is always good to develop positive relationships with media people. If by now you have identified someone in your university relations office to help you draft press releases on international events on campus, find out what their distribution network is. Is there a newspaper, radio, or TV reporter that has a special interest in international education? How about some town/gown coverage regarding international students doing service learning in the community or a host family program?

As part of your own professional development, you might want to get some training on working with the media. People who work in TV, radio, and newspaper reporting have professional standards, cultural norms, and specialized language just as international advisers do. It helps to get familiar with some of these features if you want to be seen as a trustworthy and legitimate contact for media people. For example, do you know exactly what it means to speak "on the record" and "off the record"? What about "on background" or "not for attribution"? According to the *Washington Post* (2004), "off-the-record information may not be used at all, either in the newspaper or in further reporting.... Many sources, including some officials who deal frequently with the news media, ask to go off the record when they really mean 'not for attribution to me.'" "On background" means essentially the same thing: you may attribute the information to a source by general description but not by name.

When working with the media, prepare extensively and leave as little as possible to chance. It is often helpful to provide media people with a "press kit" that contains background material on the featured event. That will save you from having to answer the same questions repeatedly—and ensures that they have the correct information. Ask in advance if you will appear on camera and what questions you are expected to answer so that you can prepare your response. Consult with the campus media office to see if they have guidance on how you should dress or if special graphics have been requested by the outside media. Some campuses require training for anyone who is likely to appear in the media because that image becomes a permanent record of how the institution presented itself to the public. If guidance is not available from any of these sources, NAFSA has a handbook for members that gives an excellent overview of how to work effectively with the media (NAFSA 2004).

Local Law Enforcement

It goes without saying that most international students and scholars are law-abiding residents in their community. However, like their domestic counterparts, they are a diverse group so you can be fairly certain that one of the international students or scholars at your campus is bound to cross paths with local law enforcement eventually. It may be a driving violation, an allegation of shop lifting, or a domestic disturbance. Be aware of and know something about each of your local law enforcement organization(s) before that happens. For example, do you know under what circumstances off-campus police authorities are called?

It's important to remember that you do not have any legal standing with regard to the incident or subsequent interactions (unless you were a victim or a perpetrator), but your office may be called on for help in arranging a translator or cultural go-between. Conversely, you may need to work cooperatively with local law enforcement in situations where international students are threatened. In the weeks following September 11, international offices all over the United

States found themselves involved in community planning to insure the safety of international students and scholars. Of great help in this was the cooperation of the campus security office. They often acted as intermediaries between campus and the community.

Bureaucratic Allies

The following agencies operate at the local community level even though they are branches of the state or national government. We have included them here because international students and scholars will encounter these bureaucracies directly in your community.

Department of Motor Vehicles (DMV)

In many states, these agencies are embroiled in the larger societal discussion about legal and illegal immigration. Helping the local DMV officials understand what documents demonstrate legal status in the United States forms a compelling alliance. You may be able to save these officials a world of trouble by introducing them to an I-20 or a DS 2019. This kind of pro-active work can mean the difference between a smooth encounter and an endless bureaucratic tangle for internationals on your campus.

Social Security Administration (SSA)

While this is a function of a much larger federal bureaucracy, the people who staff the local SSA office get little training in the fine points of immigration documents held by international students and scholars. As with the DMV, a cooperative meeting in advance of new student registration may prevent problems and make everyone's work that much easier. In the process you create a more positive environment in which international students and scholars and government officials interact.

State Allies

Local Legislators

In Chapter 2 we described some of the ways that state money flows into the coffers of colleges and universities. But it is not just dollars that matter. An hour spent with some of your state government Web sites may yield a great deal of valuable information that will help you in forming alliances. Find out what committees the state legislators for your district serve on: is there anything that touches on higher education or international issues such as trade? Find out if he/she studied abroad—would he/she be interested in speaking to a return-home event for study abroad students on your campus? Find out if he/she has an interest in a particular ethnic immigrant group in your community—maybe s/he would be willing to host an international student as part of a host family program. Do you have a graduation reception for international students as they prepare to leave the university? Could you create an "honorary citizen of your town" certificate and ask your legislator to present those certificates?

If your district legislators do not seem to be allies, branch out and find others who are. This may require some research into the members of your state legislature and how the various committee structures work. As time goes on, you may see your state legislature and the governor's office from a different perspective. As an example, we cite the decision made by the State of California to fund stem cell research done in-state. This decision creates an entirely new dimension to the relationship between higher education and the California state legislature. You may find that there are similar congruent interests in your state.

State Agencies

There may be allies tucked away in what seem to be unlikely state agencies if they have international interests on which you can capitalize. This is probably quite variable from state to state, but some possible angles to explore are offices of international trade, agriculture, tourism, or performing arts.

Federal Allies

Regardless of your type of institution, you need allies in the federal government. To briefly recap the section on federal government from Chapter 2, immigration law is federal law with oversight exercised by the Department of Homeland Security. Visas are granted by the U.S. Department of State. Here's the new element: Your congressional representatives and senators vote on all federal matters. What can you do to form alliances in this lofty arena? Whatever you do, be sure to coordinate with your campus government relations office.

Members of Congress

Every member of Congress has a staffer in his or her office who deals with immigration matters. This generally takes the form of making polite inquiries about delays in applications for an immigration benefit. Check with your boss to see if you can make these inquiries in the name of the university. Go to the congressperson's Web site. Can you find contact information for the immigration staffer? If not, simply call the office and you'll get connected. As a courtesy, ask the staffer how s/he wants to accept such inquiries (regular mail? e-mail? phone call?) Use that format consistently and respectfully.

Every member of Congress serves on a variety of committees. Some are very important; others are less so. It will not surprise you to find that the more senior members of Congress (as well as those in the majority party) serve on the most important committees. If you find that your senator or representative serves on a committee of interest to your office, start following those issues. You do not have to search this out in the newspaper—the information will be on their Web site. Once you have this knowledge, you will be in a great position to respond to calls for letters to key senators and representatives. While it may not be appropriate for you to craft the university letter on a particular subject, you may be able to provide a particularly vivid example or anecdote to the people who are writing the response. This is subtle but can be highly effective.

Members of Congress love a good media opportunity. Senators and U.S. representatives travel home often. They have a keen interest in their relationship with the colleges and universities within their districts. There's nothing quite so photogenic as an International Week festival. Both the campus media office and the elected official will be grateful for this opportunity.

Agency Allies

Department of Homeland Security

In a manner similar to bureaucracies like the DMV and the Social Security Administration, there are people who staff the local or regional offices of the Department of Homeland Security. The following are of interest in a very practical way:

➡ U.S. Citizenship and Immigration Service (USCIS)

District Office. These are the people in your community (or nearby large city) who currently deal with reinstatement applications for international students. Make a point of meeting the representatives of this office when they attend a professional conference (like NAFSA) in your region. Find out their contact information and keep it in a convenient place. If you impress them with your competence and professionalism, they will probably be more amenable to working with you toward positive solutions.

Regional Service Centers. Most applications for immigration benefits (change of status, extension of stay, etc.) are adjudicated by the USCIS Regional Service Centers. As with the District Office officials, make a point of meeting the representatives of these offices when they attend NAFSA or other professional conferences. You may be quite surprised at the level of access that is granted to representatives from colleges and universities. These polite but routinized exchanges (sometimes even by e-mail or teleconference) can prevent a multitude of problems for your office. Find out how this works in your area and plug into the system. In the long run, there may be changing patterns in how the Service Centers divide the work, but it is a good bet that you will always need to maintain good relationships with these adjudication centers.

➡ U.S. Customs and Border Protection (CBP)

This is the agency that controls local and regional airports and land borders. These are the people in your area who "inspect" and "admit" international students and scholars to the United States. Again, get their contact information and keep it on hand at all times. While you are not a party to the actual inspection and admission of internationals at the port of entry, it is your institution's documents and possibly your signature on the form that are in play. It would be helpful if your institution has had some positive and professional contact with these offices before a problem arises.

➔ U.S. Immigration and Customs Enforcement (ICE)
Generally speaking there is little interaction on a local or regional level with ICE, which is responsible for investigations of people on the wrong side of the immigration laws. The SEVIS tracking system is part of ICE and is operated from Washington, DC. However, there is always the chance that internationals on your campus may be investigated by the local/regional ICE officials. Understanding the premise of such a visit to campus is part of your job. Consult with your institution's Office of General Counsel for information on how to receive a visit from ICE or from any law enforcement agency. The good news is that you will probably not have to deal with the specifics since the attorneys for your campus should manage this process. But your graceful handling of the first contact with ICE may set the tone for an early resolution of whatever issues the ICE officials may have.

To better understand the workings of DHS and the immigration-related units, we recommend taking a tour of your closest immigration facilities. This may be at an airport where the facilities are relatively user friendly but still highly controlled. Some of the land borders include detention facilities with holding cells for those without valid documents. It is a real eye-opener to experience the culture and the work environment of border patrol units. As with your own institution, if you view federal agencies in cross-cultural terms, you have a much better opportunity to find avenues for cooperation and good communication that can, in the end, work to the benefit of international exchange.

It is a truism that the right hand of the Federal government often doesn't know what the left hand is doing. Being cynical is easy, but it is neither helpful nor professional to be snide. The Department of Homeland Security is a very new agency, constituted in the aftermath of the September 11, 2001 terrorist attacks. As it forms itself into a coherent whole, real people—agency employees, university staff, and international students—can get caught up in the works. As the SEVIS system becomes more user friendly, advisers should be guided by the highest standards of professional ethics to help one part of DHS understand how another part of that same mega-department operates. We know from our own experience that many DHS officials work as hard as we do, struggle with the changes in regulations as much we do, and care as deeply as we do about international education. It may require some patience and tongue biting, but international advisers will find that being civil and professional when working with DHS personnel will lead to much better relationships, somewhat lower stress, and possibly even better outcomes. We are not apologists for any sector of the U.S. government, but we are most certainly pragmatists about finding allies in every possible corner to support the goals of international education.

U.S. Department of State

As noted in Chapter 2, visa issuance is a function of a small part of the Department of State. The part of the U.S. embassy that issues U.S. visas is the consulate. The officials are "consular officers." Consular officers exercise an astounding amount of discretion. You may find that you become involved with an exchange of information with a particular consular officer. While you cannot ever hope to meet or get to know these individuals, you can set the tone for a polite exchange. It is important to realize that people rotate through these positions relatively frequently so you may have to revisit the training issues over and over again.

The Exchange Visitor Program (J program) is run by a small department within the Department of State. In the course of managing your institution's J program, you may exchange correspondence with the people who staff this function. Just as with other federal agencies, you can set a tone of professionalism and civility that can make the difference between a smooth exchange and a troubled one. Sometimes alliances are formed simply by being a good citizen.

A Reminder

Alliances and partnerships are an invaluable part of doing our jobs. We cannot operate without this kind of cooperation. But think carefully about the essential differences between our jobs and the jobs of those responsible for enforcing U.S. laws and regulations. International educators, regardless of the level of camaraderie with our colleagues in enforcement, are not part of that enforcement effort. Our participation in tracking international students and scholars at our institutions is defined by regulations and carefully circumscribed. It is not our job to enforce laws or regulations. It is a delicate balance to combine facilitation of international exchange with the limitations of SEVIS. Developing successful interactions with federal officials is an element in the artful creation of our profession.

Scenarios for Reflection

Now that you have a wide circle of people to consult on confusing or difficult matters, let's consider some situations we, the authors, have encountered. The goal is not to find the "correct answer," but simply to analyze and understand the multifaceted nature of the scenarios.

Imagine that you are at an informal gathering with other international advisers and notice how effectively that group can be deployed in a variety of ways.

SCENARIO **Whose Problem Is It?**

You begin: I just sat down for my first cup of tea on Monday morning and the new assistant director for Residence Life burst into my office saying, "We have to talk about one of your students." She tells me that a hall staffer got a complaint over the weekend that a male international student was seen urinating in the shower at 2:00 a.m. Now she wants me to talk to the student about his inappropriate behavior.

Adviser A: Wow, that would never happen at my school—I mean that the residence hall staff wouldn't bother me with this kind of stuff. Do you normally have a lot of interaction with them?

You: I've only been on the job a couple of months. I don't know if it's normal or not.

Adviser B: What do you know about the new assistant director? Has he or she had much experience with international students? How about the hall staffer?

You: Good question. I didn't ask. Actually, I could barely get a word in....

Adviser C: One thing you might want to find out is if the international adviser before you provided any orientation or guidance to the residence hall directors and staffers regarding international students. Maybe there's been a big turnover and this group doesn't know anything about international students. You could help out with that.

You: Good thinking.

Adviser B: Yeah, and you could ask how the hall staff normally handle complaints about student behavior. Did they follow their standard procedures with this guy? Like, did they try to find out if he was sick or drunk?

Adviser C: Bottom line, why does the assistant director think this has anything to do with you? Does she think it was a case of "cultural differences?" From where I sit, this sounds like it's the residence hall folks who have a problem, not you.

Adviser A: Good point. I'd say you need to help them become more culturally competent in initiating a discussion with students from other countries, but you probably should not call the international student into your office for a conversation about his behavior. I imagine he's familiar with the plumbing; I think he was just being lazy.

SCENARIO | **Moody or More? Consult An Expert**

Janelle begins: A student named Rachid stopped by my office to get a travel signature since he was going home over spring break. He's usually a bubbly, outgoing, successful student who likes to talk. He helped with new student orientation last year and has a wide circle of friends. I expected him to stay for a bit to chat, as he usually does, but he seemed preoccupied so I signed his I-20 and wished him good travels. He hesitated and turned to leave. When I walked out of my office a few minutes later, he was slumped in the corridor. I was talking to another student so it took me a minute wrap up with her. By the time I was finished, Rachid had left the building.

A week later, I was talking with Rachid's girl friend and asked her about him. She avoided my question. A few days after that, I was in a planning meeting for International Week and someone asked if Rachid was going to take the lead on the Moroccan table as he had before. One of his fellow students says curtly, "Not likely."

I don't want to be too nosy about him, but I'm worried that Rachid may be having some kind of problem. How would you folks approach this situation?

Adviser B: Well, changes in behavior can be signals but your gut instinct about jumping in too soon seems wise to me. Have you thought about what kind of assumptions you may be making?

Janelle: Hmmm, well, so far I can only assume that something isn't right. And evidently other people have noticed or maybe they even know what's going on.

Adviser D: You might try pumping the friends for information, but it might be better to consult with someone in your Counseling Center to figure out a strategy. These kinds of situations can be really tricky.

Janelle: Yeah, I really don't feel prepared to deal with mental health issues—not my area of strength at all!

Adviser A: Hey, it's not supposed to be your strong suit. You're an international adviser, not a shrink. The most you can reasonably do is try to steer Rachid to someone who really can help, whether that's a counselor or even his parents.

FOLLOW-UP ACTIVITIES

1. Create a networking schedule for yourself. Look at your calendar and find the relatively less busy times when you can arrange meetings with all of the people we have identified in this chapter. It could easily take you a year to make contacts and establish good relations with people on your campus and in your community.
2. Based on your campus contacts make a list of potential "programming partners" for the international office. Add at least one new one this year. Use your imagination.
3. Read your local newspaper(s). Notice the names of reporters who cover higher education and international topics.
4. Locate and attend meetings of your local NAFSA network.
5. Arrange and/or participate in a tour of the nearest port of entry for international students and scholars.
6. Visit the nearest DHS/CIS office to see exactly where students have to go for certain services.
7. Learn something about the state legislator(s) who represents the district where your institution is located and his/her relationship with your institution.
8. Put the names and contact information for your two U.S. senators and congressional representative for the district where your institution is located in a handy place where you can always find it.
9. Go to your senators' and representative's Web sites and find out what committees they sit on. Places to start: http://www.house.gov/writerep/ and http://www.senate.gov/general/contact_information/senators_cfm.cfm

Works Cited and Resources

Burak, Patricia and William Hoffa, eds. 2001. *Crisis Management in a Cross-Cultural Setting*. Washington, DC: NAFSA Association of International Educators.

Institute of International Education. 2005. *Open Doors: Report on International Educational Exchange*. New York.

NAFSA: Association of International Educators. 2004. *Working with the News Media: A Different Kind of Advocacy*. Washington, DC.

The National Center for Education Statistics (NCES), February 18, 2006. Retrieved from http://nces.ed.gov/ipeds/

Rosser, Vicki J., Jill M. Hermsen, Ketevan Mamiseishvili, and Melinda S. Wood. Forthcoming January 2007. "The Impact of SEVIS on U.S. International Student and Scholar Advisors." *Higher Education: The International Journal of Higher Education and Planning*. Dordrecht: Springer Netherlands.

U.S. Department of State, www.state.gov

Washington Post, March 7, 2004. "For the Record, What It All Means," p. B05. www.washingtonpost.com

YOUR NOTES

BECOMING AN EFFECTIVE ADVOCATE

CHAPTER 4

By now you should have a much better sense of your professional environment and who you can turn to for various kinds of assistance whether at the campus, community, state, or federal level. Hopefully, these allies in your network have realized that you are a trusted and helpful resource for them as well. We now encourage you to think one step ahead. Rather than focusing just on solving problems, this chapter will help you develop strategies to prevent problems. This is part of being an advocate. You may not feel like carrying the flag for international education every day, but we very strongly believe that we must use our networks of allies to advance the benefits of international education.

What Does "Advocacy" Mean?

According to the Encarta dictionary, advocacy is defined as "giving aid to a cause." That is pretty much what we do everyday when we help students to navigate the U.S. academic system and local culture. Beyond aiding the individual, however, advocacy is embedded in a political framework that is more clearly articulated in synonyms such as "backing" or "sponsorship." Advocating for international education requires a political mindset that enables one to participate in a wide array of advocacy activities and enlist others as allies in the cause.

"Oh, yuck," you may be saying right now. "I hate politics." Some people find it more palatable to think of politics as a form of diplomacy, which is a form of cross-cultural communication. You pride yourself on your cross-cultural competence, so this is a chance to exercise those skills in a different way. In different political times, these skills and the necessity for this kind of work were far less important because international students were viewed as academic and cultural assets, or at the very least, as sources of increased revenue, much needed labor, or campus diversity. International advisers and students have weathered other bad political times, such as the Iran hostage crisis of the late 1970s and spy charges against Chinese researchers, but when terrorists set off bombs in the World Trade Center in 1993 and one of them was allegedly "on an expired student visa" (technically he was out-of-status, but what do the media know about immigration terminology?), the tide began turning. In the mid-1990s, the pilot program for SEVIS was rolled out in several southeastern states as a test. Then the attacks on September 11, 2001 happened and the rush was on to close the gates against terrorists who were portrayed as lining up at U.S. embassies and consulates abroad with fistfuls of I-20s in hand. International educators knew that student visas were already among the most closely scrutinized visa categories, but the public perception was different.

This is exactly why all of us must engage in politics: to advocate for international students and for international education in general. By "politics" we mean not only the formal processes of governmental decisionmaking, but also the informal processes of identifying issues of common cause and bringing about change. It is no longer enough simply to enjoy international students, to help them, to spend time with host families and others who share the same views, to hold hands and sing folk songs. We must collectively work to change public perceptions about international students and to educate those in public office about the benefits of international education.

Most people who are involved with international students and scholars in a sustained way eventually become outspoken advocates for this population. If you do not really enjoy working with people who are in the midst of changing languages and/or cultures or you do not believe that international education benefits your campus and community, it is nearly impossible to advocate effectively for the individuals or the cause. If you do not want to participate in advocacy work in any way, shape, or form, it may be time to go back to Chapter 1 to reassess your goals and values as they relate to your career choices. If you don't feel prepared for the task, but are willing to learn and to strap on your armor to go to battle for something you really believe in, this chapter is a start in preparing you.

Campus Advocacy

Let's start small. One of the first and best places to begin advocating for international students is on your campus. In addition to the alliance-building activities we suggested in Chapter 3, there are some clear advocacy steps you can take. If you have experienced the same kind of problem several times, you can offer to spearhead a committee or taskforce to find a solution to the problem. Consider the following situation.

SCENARIO	**Confusing Language**

Over time you have had numerous conversations with international students and scholars about the taxes and other items that are withheld from their paychecks. You help them understand the basic structure of why the university must do this withholding and how the U.S. government collects taxes in this manner. But you don't have complete information about the various abbreviations that appear on the paycheck stub. For example, international students and scholars are puzzled by items such as "SS" or "FIT" or "LTD."

You have an informational interview with the Payroll Office to "translate" the ten most common payroll deductions. You also talk with them about how they answer similar questions from other new hires. After realizing that many new employees have the same questions, your offices jointly produce a handout in easy-to-understand language and the Payroll Office agrees to put the handout in their information packet for all new employees. By bringing this matter to their attention and helping them to find a solution, you've helped not only the international students and scholars at your campus, but you've streamlined your own work and the work of the Payroll Office, and you've helped other employees as well.

This kind of small action is good preparation for a larger look at campus advocacy. To begin, get a copy of the most recent campus Strategic Plan and review the priorities. It is quite possible that international education is listed somewhere, but it may not be getting the support it needs. You can provide that push. If there is no mention of anything international in the Strategic Plan, you have a couple of options. Find a goal, objective, or priority that sounds like it could include international education and international students ("increasing diversity" is a good bet). Find out what unit on campus has primary responsibility for implementing that item and make contact with them. Can you align some part of your office activities with the target and help them to meet the goal? This is a great way to create allies while advocating for your own interests. If your campus is going to develop a new strategic plan, volunteer (with your boss's permission) to be on the committee. Senior faculty and staff have probably been through this exercise several times, so the chances you will be selected are pretty good. This is also a great way to get to know other people on campus and find out what their big issues are.

Community Advocacy

As we noted in Chapter 3, your allies in the local community can be excellent advocates for international education and the concerns of international students and scholars. They may be perceived as more "purely" motivated in their intentions whereas you may be seen as self-serving in that your advocacy work ensures your continued employment. Also, volunteers are free to say whatever they like so they can turn up the emotional or political heat in ways that you may not feel are appropriate for you as a representative of your institution. Where you may be limited by your position on campus, they can orchestrate campaigns to write letters to the editors of local papers, organize civic drives, and call upon their own networks of community people for support of particular issues. For example, if international students are having trouble getting a driver's license and you are having no luck with the DMV, perhaps some of the local friendship families have more influential contacts in the local bureaucracy or know an elected official who can help to change procedures. You won't know until you reach out to all parts of your allies network.

We cannot stress enough the value of local news media in your advocacy work. Local news forms a bridge between your community advocacy and advocacy at the state and national level. You may not think your local TV or newspaper reporters are very good, but their reach is wide. Many TV news programs are broadcast statewide and get the attention of state legislators in districts far removed from yours. Your local newspapers are probably available online and are read faithfully by your congressional delegation or their staff members, both in the local offices and in Washington. According to a 2002 study, Washington insiders (elected and appointed officials, staff, lobbyists, media, and other Capitol Hill employees) are "news junkies" and spend one to five hours a day engaged in some form of news collection (Atlantic Media Research and Hart 2002). While much of their focus is on news generated in Washington rather than back home, congressional staff members are particularly concerned about getting the facts and background information as well as understanding the positions of advocacy groups. You can provide a small measure of such information by getting stories or letters into your local news media.

State and National Advocacy

International advisers who participate in advocacy work at this level of government generally have positive experiences. The key to success is good preparation. Study your issues and study your target audience. There is a wealth of information available about your local and national representatives on the Internet. You may be surprised to find that one of your state legislators has been a host to an international high school student or that one of your senators' aides studied abroad in college. A few key tips on getting your message across are:

- ➡ Provide background information and facts; do it in a short and succinct manner (don't bury them with data).
- ➡ Build on the relationship by providing periodic updates or additional information.
- ➡ Don't assume the person you are talking to knows about or cares about your issue.
- ➡ Give them a local-specific reason to care about your issue.
- ➡ Send a follow-up note of thanks and provide any information they request.

It is vital to remember that international advisers are not professional lobbyists when they advocate for international education. Some campuses retain the services of lobbyists, but .are most effective when we speak from the strength of our convictions as committed citizens. We need to know who is indeed lobbying on behalf of higher education in the United States and how we can tie our issues to theirs, but it's important to realize that members of Congress listen to their voting constituents differently than they listen to paid lobbyists.

The Role of the "Big Six" Associations in National Higher Education

Higher education institutions have come late to the federal table, or should we say trough (to capitalize on the "pork" analogy), of political advocacy. Historically, colleges and universities stayed out of the political process for the most part until the 1970s when they began using the major higher education member associations to lobby on their behalf; only since the 1990s have they become a major force in shaping higher education policy (Cook 1998). The coalition known as the "Big Six" comprises the following member associations (listed in the order used by Cook):

- ACE: American Council on Education (formed 1918). Membership is open to all higher education institutions.
- AAU: Association of American Universities (formed 1900). Membership is by invitation, primarily graduate and research institutions, both public and private. AAU is known informally as the "presidential" organization, i.e., its members are the presidents of the universities.
- AASCU: American Association of State Colleges and Universities (formed 1961). Membership is open to all public bachelor and graduate degree-granting institutions.
- NASULGC: National Association of State Universities and Land-Grant Colleges (formed 1887). Membership comprises state and land-grant universities.
- NAICU: National Association of Independent Colleges and Universities (formed 1976). Membership is limited to private institutions.
- AACC: American Association of Community Colleges (formed 1992). Membership is open to two-year degree-granting colleges.

Higher education institutions are encouraged to hold membership in ACE, and they may also join one or two of the other associations (Cook 1998). Each of the associations takes the lead on issues that are most important to its membership while ACE serves a coordinating function among the six. The Big Six also meet regularly with other policy associations including the Association of Community College Trustees, the Association of Catholic Colleges and Universities, the Association of Governing Boards, the Association of Jesuit Colleges and Universities, the Council of Independent Colleges, the Hispanic Association of Colleges and Universities, the National Association of College and University Business Officers, the National Association for Equal Opportunity in Higher Education, the National Association of Student Financial Aid Administrators, and the United Negro College Fund. Another group of approximately 24 associations meet with ACE less frequently.

NAFSA: Association of International Educators is the primary member association for international advisers as well as individuals involved in the other parts of the international exchange enterprise. Similar to the Big Six, NAFSA participates in the Alliance for International Educational and Cultural Exchange, which comprises 80 other associations in international education including People to People International, Sister Cities International, YMCA International, and many of the student exchange programs for high school and college students (www.alliance-exchange.org). These groups often work together to determine who will take the lead on various issues and how to conduct the most effective advocacy efforts on issues such as immigration reform, foreign language study, and so on. The individual organizations also have their own priorities and strategies to achieve their goals. NAFSA hosts an Advocacy Day each year, which enables international education leaders to meet with their congressional delegations in Washington, DC. To facilitate letter-writing campaigns, NAFSA has a Take Action Center on its Web site that provides members with sample letters to personalize and send to their members of Congress. Additionally, NAFSA has a program called Advocacy Centered Team (ACT) where members can register to receive alerts to contact their legislators on issues related to international education.

Current Issues in U.S. Higher Education

It is always useful to know where your issues fit in the big picture. The Association of Governing Boards of Universities and Colleges (2005) noted the following concerns for U.S. higher education in 2005 and 2006.

1. Homeland security (no change from 2003/04)
2. Scientific research (up from #9 in 2003/04)
3. The price of tuition (up from #5 in 2003/04)
4. Participation of low-income students
5. Diminishing state capacity for setting higher education policy
6. The culture wars
7. Economic and workforce development
8. Accountability to the public
9. Ownership of intellectual property
10. Aftereffects of Sarbanes-Oxley

Which of these issues has anything to do with international education, in either a negative or positive way? Clearly the work we do in bringing international students and scholars to the United States is considered to be a negative to those who worry that all internationals have the potential to jeopardize homeland security. Regardless of how often international educators have tried to correct media reports on how many of the World Trade Center terrorists of 1993 and 2001 were alleged to be here on student visas, that information has not gotten nearly as much media coverage as the incorrect or poorly written stories. SEVIS is one outcome of this dearly held misperception. Given the supposed negative implications for our work, advisers are usually reminded to modulate their criticisms of SEVIS and related issues lest they appear to be unconcerned with homeland security, the top issue on the list. More recently, the debate has begun shifting, and policymakers are realizing that international students and scholars are part of the solution to terrorism—not part of the problem.

Regarding scientific research (#2 on the list), international students and scholars make up a significant portion of the scientific research community so we can consider our work in getting them here to be a positive. Problems with post-September 11 visa delays abroad have created quite a stir at many research universities that rely on a steady stream of graduate students and post-doctoral scholars from all over the world to complete federally funded research projects. With NAFSAns having long-heralded the cry to fix the visa system, we can be heartened that associations such as National Academy of Sciences and the National Academy of Engineering have taken up the charge for visa reform in Congress.[1]

In the price of tuition (#3), international students are an almost wholly positive factor. Because the majority of international students rely on personal or family funds to cover the costs of their education (Institute of International Education 2005) and they must provide evidence of sufficient funding to obtain a student visa, they are a relatively low financial risk for colleges and universities. Barring national or large scale natural disasters, international students tend to maintain full-time enrollment, pay their tuition (usually at non-resident rates) on time, and manage to scrape up funds when tuition goes up, unlike their U.S. counterparts who can drop out or go part-time when finances are tight. Thus international students can be a source of financial stability for their institutions.

Depending on one's perspective, international education might be viewed as either a negative or a positive in relation to some of the other seven issues. For example, do international students contribute to the culture wars (#6) simply by their presence in the United States (a visible reminder to immigration foes who think that diversity has already gone too far), or are they peace ambassadors who can enrich Americans' understanding of the world? Are they taking away slots from otherwise qualified American students who might need financial aid to afford higher education (#4)? Are they perceived to be staying in the United States after they graduate and taking away jobs from citizens or driving down wages (#7) in spite of evidence to

[1]Four organizations comprise the Academies: the National Academy of Sciences, the National Academy of Engineering, the Institute of Medicine, and the National Research Council.

the contrary (Anderson 1996)? Are they a boon to the development of intellectual property or are they stealing ideas for other countries to use against U.S. interests (#9)? According to the Alexis de Tocqueville Institution (Peters 1996), *one of every four* U.S. patents is created by immigrants or by immigrants collaborating with U.S.-born co-inventors. And just *what is* Sarbanes-Oxley (#10) and how does it figure in anything we do? We may know visa regulations, but most of us don't know much about accounting. In a nutshell, Sarbanes-Oxley has to do with reforming corporate governance rules, financial disclosures, and accounting practices. We'd be willing to bet that your campus' Vice President for Administration or Finance cares *a lot* about this.

Vartan Gregorian, quoted at the beginning of Chapter 2, identified a slightly different set of most-pressing issues in higher education. The top five issues he identified are:

1. Maintaining academic freedom while conducting research.
   His concern is that federal and commercial interests may compromise research endeavors.
2. Providing intellectual coherence in the information revolution.
   Massive amounts of available information have led to fragmentation and excessive specialization of knowledge.
3. Facing the economic challenges that come with greater access.
   As more attend colleges and universities, the share that students pay is likely to grow.
4. Keeping pace with international competition.
   Other regions and countries are adapting their academic programs and competing for part of the U.S. market.
5. Taking more responsibility for K-12 education.
   Higher education needs to address the problems of K-12 education and do more to better train teachers.

Whether positive or negative, you can be fairly certain that someone in your institutional leadership, state legislature, and congressional delegation is thinking about these issues. If you can find a way to tie your concerns to what has already captured their attention, your story has a better chance of being heard.

At the national level, there is a particular nexus forming between concerns about America losing its economic and scientific edge and the participation of international students and scholars in scientific research in the United States. If you begin to tune into this discussion, you will develop a voice on this important national issue. You can begin this research by looking at the article by Lemonick (2006) listed at the end of this chapter.

Finding Your Advocacy Voice

If you are interested in writing song lyrics, you first have to listen to a lot of music. If you are interested in writing a love letter, it helps to pay attention to poetry. If you are interested in writing a letter that might actually make a difference in international education, then first read ones that have made a difference.

Start with the person on your campus who deals with government relations. Listen to their take on international education issues; read what your institution has written in the past, even if it is on a different topic. Don't be discouraged if your campus has never commented on any issue pertaining to international students. You can become a resource for them and work with them to craft their first advocacy efforts in this area.

NAFSA has a number of resources to help its members become more comfortable with advocacy efforts at the national level. They have a great handbook with ideas on how to most effectively communicate with your members of Congress and that explains how Congress establishes laws and the role that constituents can play in the lawmaking process (see Resources at the end of this chapter). It also explains some of the arcane terminology used by legislators and lists who sits on which committees that affect international education so you don't have to research all this for yourself. NAFSA's Web site offers you another option for advocating; they have sample letters posted that you can individualize and then e-mail directly to your congressional delegation. NAFSA also has a network of state "whips" in key states (i.e., they have senators and representatives who sit on committees that make decisions on higher education); if you live in one of these states, your "whip" will contact you and provide sample letters for you to follow.

The most important note to hit when using your advocacy voice is the personal note: highlight the impact that a particular decision will have on your campus (direct student or faculty effects) and the things that matter to your institution. A recent survey published by the Congressional Management Foundation (Fitch and Goldschmidt 2005) found that members of Congress and their staffers are likely to rate e-mail that has a personalized message or story as "very important" 47 percent of the time whereas a generic "blast" e-mail message is rated as "very important" only about 3 percent of the time. So make your message count! If you work at an institution that focuses on agricultural research and your government liaison has extensive cooperative research agreements with institutions in the developing world, you may be able to offer a vivid and meaningful anecdote (e.g. based on a visa nightmare that a sub-Saharan student at your campus encountered) that could be a part of a larger institutional response on visa problems. If you work at an institution that focuses on music performance, you may find that your issues resonate most deeply (pun intended) in the context of problems experienced by international performers coming to your campus.

Institutional Versus Individual Advocacy

Before engaging in any advocacy activities you need to find out if there are any institutional policies regarding who may contact legislative entities on governmental matters. On some campuses such communications must be vetted through the government relations office or the president's office. Other institutions have a policy that prohibits employees from engaging in any advocacy efforts. This does not mean that you have to remain completely silent. We have found that the appropriate "higher-ups" are often willing to sign letters that we drafted on their behalf; however, their willingness came about only because we had nurtured our relationships with them and had proven ourselves well-informed and trustworthy. This is the happy pay-off for doing your homework in Chapters 2 and 3.

As a separate matter, as a private citizen you have a right to express your individual views on any governmental matter you find important. You can direct your comments to your state legislators and congressional delegation as you wish—and do not let anyone try to convince you otherwise (sadly, we do know of individuals who are so intimidated by their superiors that they do not feel empowered to exercise their Constitutional right to free speech even outside of work). If you have concerns of this nature, you may be relieved to know that quite often when you telephone a legislator's office, you will not be asked for your name. You can simply say, "I am a constituent of Representative X and I encourage her to support the bill to increase funding for . . ...." If you choose to put your comments in writing as a private citizen, do *not* use your office or institutional letterhead. Also, do *not* use your office computer to send e-mail or faxes unless you have checked your institutional policies and state laws regarding personal use of institutional equipment. Otherwise, you may find yourself reprimanded, fired, or even charged with a criminal act.

You may find that you cross district boundaries on your commute to work (both state and federal districts can be very strangely shaped). This in effect doubles your opportunities to advocate for international education, an advocacy "two-fer" as it were. You can write first as a private citizen to those who represent your residential area and you can also have your government liaison (or whoever else communicates on behalf of the institution) write from the campus' district.

Your personal advocacy efforts will be most effective if you are registered to vote and participate in the electoral process regularly. You should know where candidates stand on international education and vote for those whose positions you support. When you write or call and say, "I voted for you in the past three elections and now you have changed your view on visa reform, so I will have to change my vote next year," that will most certainly get their attention.

FOLLOW-UP ACTIVITIES

1. Get a copy of your campus Strategic Plan and read it if you have not already done so. Is there any mention of international education, especially incoming or outbound students?
2. Read a sample advocacy letter with a goal of writing one advocacy letter (either personal or institutional) within the next six months. NAFSA makes these available on their Web site at www.nafsa.org/takeaction.
3. Register to vote. Then vote. If you move, even within the same state, make sure that you reregister to vote if you have changed congressional districts, counties, or other municipalities.
4. State: In addition to having the name(s) and contact information for the legislator(s) who represent the district in which your campus is located, if you live in a different district, get the name(s) and contact information for the legislator(s) who represent the district in which you reside.
5. State: Get the names and contact information for members of the legislative committees that deal with higher education, international trade, and other pertinent issues.
6. Find out which of the "Big Six" associations your institution belongs to and who on your campus is the liaison to those associations.
7. Federal: If you live in a different district than the one in which your campus is located, get the name and contact information for the House member who represents the district in which you reside. (see www.nafsa.org/takeaction)
8. Register for NAFSA's Advocacy Centered Team (ACT) at www.nafsa.org/act to receive action alerts on legislation related to international education and exchange.

Works Cited and Resources

Anderson, Stuart. 1996. "The Wage and Employment Impact of Immigrant Scientists and Engineers in High Technology." *International Educator*, Vol. VI, No. 1, p. 27–32.

Atlantic Media Research, and Peter D. Hart Research Associates. 2002. *Washington in the Information Age*.

Association of Governing Boards of Universities and Colleges. 2005. "Ten Public Policy Issues for Higher Education in 2005 and 2006." AGB *Public Policy Paper Series*, Washington, DC.

Cook, Constance E. 1998. *Lobbying for Higher Education: How Colleges and Universities Influence Federal Policy*. Nashville: Vanderbilt University Press.

Fitch, Brad, and Kathy Goldschmidt. 2005. *Communicating with Congress. How Capitol Hill Is Coping with the Surge in Citizen Advocacy*. Washington, DC: Congressional Management Foundation.

Gregorian, Vartan. 2005. "Leading Today's Colleges and Universities: Challenges and Opportunities." *The Presidency*,Vol. 8, No. 2, p. 29–33.

Institute of International Education. 2005. *Open Doors: Report on International Educational Exchange*. New York: Institute of International Education.

Lemonick, Michael. "Are We Losing Our Edge?" *Time Magazine*, February 13, 2006, www.time.com/time/archive/preview/0,10987,1156575,00.html (accessed February 28, 2006).

NAFSA: Association of International Educators. 2006. Advocacy Handbook. www.nafsa.org/_/Document/_/advocacy_handbook.pdf

NAFSA: Association of International Educators. 2006. Take Action Center. www.nafsa.org/public_policy.sec/public_policy_priorities

Peters, Philip. 1996. "Invented in the USA: Immigrants, Patents, and Jobs." Report of a study conducted by the Alexis de Tocqueville Institution, New York.

UNDERSTANDING PROFESSIONALISM AND EMBRACING COMPLEXITY

CHAPTER 5

In previous chapters we mentioned the importance of professional and ethical behavior. We trust that you have a general sense of what these terms mean. In fact, the notions of professionalism and ethics have been studied extensively by scholars in many disciplines. We cannot cover the whole map of this terrain, but it is vital that you develop a more sophisticated understanding of what the terms mean in your current work setting.

This chapter looks more closely at what it means to be a professional and what it means to behave in an ethical manner. We also present some complicated scenarios drawn from real situations for you to consider. These scenarios will begin to integrate some of the activities from the previous chapters in a way that will challenge your thinking and will confuse you. We have included a number of straightforward suggestions to help you organize your thought processes. We recommend that you work through the sections with colleagues and perhaps your supervisor. You will probably discover a range of viable responses to the situations.

What Constitutes a Profession

International advising is a specialized field that is not particularly well known or understood even within higher education. When we compare ourselves to colleagues who work in financial aid, the registrar's office, admissions, housing or other areas, we should ask if our field is indeed a profession or is it just another highly technical cog in the paper-pushing bureaucracy of higher education as some would assert? Is our professionalism conferred merely by dint of our close association with professors and other academics in higher education? To be a profession, we need to be more than the beneficiaries of a spillover effect; we need to meet the benchmarks of professionalism.

Professional status is usually conferred on an occupation that has several characteristics. Among them are:

1. A specialized body of knowledge based on theory as well as practice;
2. A required period of education and training, usually at the university level;
3. Client service is central to practitioners;

4. Practitioners have a high level of personal commitment to the field;
5. Practitioners share a set of values that contribute to a sense of shared identity;
6. The values of the occupation have a relationship to broader social values shared by people outside the field;
7. A binding code of ethics that derive from those values;
8. A means of self-regulation, often through codes of ethics, standards of professional practice, licensure or certification (Pemberton 1991, 1992).

Is International Advising a Profession?

So how does international advising measure up as a profession in light of these features? By and large, international advisers are very client centered and have a deep commitment to the work they do (Rosser et al. forthcoming 2007). Many advisers are either members of NAFSA: Association of International Educators or participate in NAFSA activities; this involvement helps to establish a sense of shared identity and a common set of values among advisers. NAFSA also has a code of ethics and a statement of principles that support professional behavior among members. Although we do not regulate one another *per se* (e.g., sanctioning by licensure revocation), we rely heavily on our shared values and professional standards to monitor our practices especially in critical areas such as accepting DSO or RO (Designated School Official and Responsible Officer) authority on behalf of our campuses.

With regard to items 1 and 2, specialized bodies of knowledge are most definitely needed, notably interpreting federal regulations and communicating across cultural differences, but no specific formal education or training is in fact required prior to becoming an international adviser. Virtually no single academic path addresses the core theories and skills needed to become an international adviser, though some institutions have developed degree programs for aspiring international advisers (Dessoff 2006). Other options include earning a degree in intercultural communications or law, but neither of these paths is quite sufficient by itself. Most international student advisers hold bachelor or master degrees that relate in one way or another to their work (Rosser et al. forthcoming 2007). At the same time, it is also true that some advisers have worked their way up from secretarial positions while others have been faculty with Ph.D.s.

Given this lack of a clear academic program that delivers the necessary body of theory and practice, one may wonder what the purpose of a baccalaureate or advanced degree is for becoming an international adviser. There are probably many answers to this question, but with regard to the nature of professionalism, one answer may be that the fundamental value of a liberal arts education in general prepares one to think as a professional. That is, the individual learns to read and think with a critical perspective, to communicate complex ideas verbally and in writing, to frame events in a broader context, to seek more information, to operate from theoretical perspectives rather than from anecdotes, and to ask meaningful questions. The benefit is in developing the mindset that allows for subsequent skill building. Thus, what is missing in the wide range of academic disciplines that can lead to the profession of international advising is structured skills development. While many advisers and other university administrators may think it is sufficient to learn their professional skills on the job, consider how one would react if this logic were applied to the better established professions of medicine, law, or education: "Sure, go ahead and practice on me/my loved one. I'm confident that your academic knowledge is enough." Somehow, we think not. This missing training component may be the weak link in arguing for international advising as a profession.

Another attribute of professions that might be lacking in international advising is item #6, values that have a relationship to broader social values shared by people outside the field. At the time of this writing, U.S. policy statements indicate support for international interchange (according to current Secretary of State Condoleeza Rice and Undersecretary of State Karen Hughes) and higher education in general but government practice and public opinion are lagging behind. Higher education is currently viewed as a personal benefit rather than a public good, resulting in state support being redirected to other state priorities such as health care and prisons. Colleges and universities are being forced to re-examine their priorities and it is hard to see how "our" values regarding person-to-person diplomacy and global understanding are part of a greater value system these days.

This scenario stands in contrast to the situation just a few years earlier when international student enrollments were rising annually and "internationalization" was a highly desirable goal on campuses large and small. International students and scholars contributed to campus coffers and classrooms, supported research projects and campus diversity efforts, and some stayed on to build the high tech revolution of the 1990s. All of these activities are considered suspect by those who want to secure our borders from worrisome aliens both documented and undocumented, thus making our values seem dangerously naive rather than thoughtfully professional.

In sum, it is evident that international advising, like many mid-level administrative careers in colleges and universities shares many of the traits of a profession. How to manage shifting societal values regarding international education is not entirely within the control of advisers. Thus the only professional characteristic that we may be able to directly influence is the need for formal training prior to entry in the field. With the guidance of NAFSA and other professional associations, more degree programs are being established and comprehensive professional training programs are available to new advisers.

Regardless of the formal definitions of "profession," however, international advisers should be encouraged by the following statement from Kegan (1994), "What it means to be 'professional' might have less to do with external social definitions than with internal psychological capacity" (p. 158). That is, having the mindset and skills to think like a professional is much more important than how others define our work. We will come back to these issues in the next chapter.

Professionalism, Ethical Conduct, and Codes of Ethics

There are broad ethical principles that form the foundation for most professional codes of ethics. We strongly suggest you become familiar with NAFSA's Code of Ethics (provided in Appendix B), especially the section on advising international students and scholars. Of course you should follow these professional standards. But be warned, if you decide to rely merely on the strictures outlined in the Code, you will be only partially prepared to deal with the truly difficult ethical situations that you are bound to encounter in your career. If you haven't gone into an ethnic restaurant and been waited on by an international student who is clearly working without permission, just wait. You will eventually. If someone at your campus (a professor, dean, or vice-president, perhaps) hasn't informed you that s/he just reported an international student to some branch of the federal government, just wait. It will happen. For these gut-wrenching reasons, international advisers need a solid grounding in ethics that goes beyond simple yes/no guidance.

First, it helps to be clear on the difference between what is legal, what is ethical, and what is moral. These words are often used interchangeably but they actually delineate very different spheres of applicability. Kitchener (2000) defines morals as "what people believe about what is right and wrong or good and bad about character or conduct (p. 2). Laws are rules of conduct that are codified, have sanctions or consequences for their violation, and can vary from place to place. Interestingly, Kitchener notes that just because something is a law, it "does not necessarily specify an ethical obligation" (p. 5) for taking action. We will return to this notion later in the chapter. Ethics is a branch of philosophy that examines morality and "addresses questions of how people ought to act toward each other" (p. 2); it is in this prescriptive context that ethical codes for professions have been developed.

Ethical Principles

Kitchener (1984, 2000) identified five core principles as a foundation for ethical decision-making. These principles form the basis for many professional codes of ethics. They are:

1. *Respect autonomy*. This assumes that the person being given autonomy is rational and competent. The absence of either rationality or competence or both may lead to a decision based on one of the other principles. In general, it is safe to assume that if an international student or scholar has made their way through multiple academic and governmental bureaucracies and ended up at your institution, they have at least a modicum of rationality and competence.
2. *Benefiting others*. This should be balanced with autonomy and should not be used as an excuse for paternalism. There are a number of very "old school" international advisers who have a hard time balancing the first and second principles (okay, some don't even try). They tend to have a paternalistic view of internationals as being incompetent and in need of "help." However, the help they proffer can be intrusive, unwelcome, or even detrimental (see principle 3). This type of well-intended effort, in fact, violates the first principle of autonomy. The key notion here is *balancing these two principles*.
3. *Do no harm*. This holds a stronger obligation than benefiting others, so if a decision is meant to benefit someone but could in fact harm them, the best decision is to do no harm. In terms of international advising, this includes the notion that you should not raise expectations when you don't know what the outcome will be. Even simple platitudes such as, "I'm sure we can find some way to work out this problem," carry the potential for harm when the problem happens to be about a person's non-immigrant status and you don't control the decision process. What you offer merely as words of comfort, in fact, overstates your ability to solve the problem. There are sound ethical principles that teach doctors to use much more measured expressions like, "We're doing everything we can to help your son/daughter/mother."
4. *Being just*. This is based on fairness, equality, impartiality, or reciprocity. This principle may play out very differently in different cultures, so may be most troubling to apply in cross-cultural settings. For example, in cultures where age is a critical measure of status, it is appropriate to be deferential to whoever is older. In the culture of U.S. higher education, however, age is less important than position (e.g., rank or class), so if a young adviser addresses an older graduate student from an age-status country by first name, the student is likely to be surprised and possibly even offended. One way in which position clearly trumps age in U.S. higher education is in the course registration system—graduate students get to register for classes before undergraduates, seniors before juniors, and so on.

5. *Being faithful.* This involves loyalty, truthfulness, keeping promises, and respect.

Ethical dilemmas occur when two or more ethical principles come into conflict. The subsequent difficulty in deciding what to do is not because the principles are not clear, but precisely because they *are* clear. The dilemma is in finding a course of action that least violates the principles. In situations such as, "I pushed him out the window to save him from the fire, but he died from the ten-story fall," the principle of doing no harm was violated by trying to follow the principle of benefiting others. Thus international advisers can use these principles as well as NAFSA's Code of Ethics when faced with ethical dilemmas such as those described earlier.

Gary Althen (1995), a former NAFSA president, offers a more concrete set of guiding questions an adviser can ask themselves when making decisions with ethical implications. He suggests:

1. Is the proposed decision in harmony with the letter of relevant laws, regulations, and institutional policies?
2. Is it in harmony with the spirit of pertinent laws, regulations, and policies?
3. Does it comply with the NAFSA Code of Ethics?
4. Is it in accord with cultural norms?
5. Does it avoid duplicity?
6. Is it consistent with decisions previously made in comparable cases, and/or distinguishable from previous cases in which a different decision was reached?
7. Does it establish a desirable precedent?
8. Does it avoid lines of thought that can easily lead off the correct path:
   a. If I don't do it, someone else will.
   b. It's not worth the hassle.
   c. I could lose my job if I did (or didn't) do what has been asked.
9. Will it help in the long run?
10. Would the world be a better place if this decision is taken? If more people made this decision?
11. Does it feel right? Would it bring me more self-respect?
12. Considering my personal feeling toward the person or group that would be affected by my proposed decision: Would I make the same decision if it affected someone I liked or disliked?
13. Would I want my mother to know I made this decision?
14. Could I credibly defend this decision in public?
15. If I were the one affected by the proposed decision, would I consider it fair and reasonable?
16. Would I want to read about it in the newspaper?

Implications for Decisionmaking and the Exercise of Discretion

At the campus level, advisers are given varying degrees of latitude to define their roles and responsibilities and to structure how they will accomplish the work they do. For example, some advisers have a free hand in establishing the content and format for new student orientations. Other advisers play a small role in orientation because someone else is responsible for planning and conducting that activity. Advisers may have little control over when and how they interact with students or they may be encouraged to set their own schedule and jump into handling regulatory cases right away.

How much or how little discretion you can exercise may be dictated by a number of factors. How much experience do you have? How firm is your grasp of technical details? Have you demonstrated a capacity to think critically in complex situations? Has your supervisor encouraged you to push your limits? Does your supervisor trust your judgment based on prior decisions you have made? Can you distill problems into key issues and describe them clearly? How are your habits of documentation and consultation? Is your boss a control freak?

As you become a more competent professional, demonstrating that you operate within the values and behaviors of the profession, you can be expected to engage in a greater degree of self-regulation. This involves developing a higher order ability to make decisions and exercise discretion in both the small and the large aspects of your job. This is harder than you might think. For most people, it requires a shift in attitude from being a follower to being willing to take the risk to become a decisionmaker in your office, on your campus, or in the profession.

Because of the lack of training during the academic preparation of international advisers (described above), the actual work of international advising provides an extraordinary training ground for the development of these skills and abilities. It begins with the puzzle of how some relatively small issue fits into immigration law and regulation and, simultaneously, how it fits into institutional policy. It ends with consideration of how national policy fits into the higher goals of international cooperation and world peace.

Process of Ethical Decisionmaking

There are a number of steps in decisionmaking, all of which push us towards a better and more responsible understanding of the exercise of discretion. This is not to say that every decision must go through the steps in lock-step fashion. You may find that you are a highly intuitive and that you are not aware of any step-by-step process in your decisionmaking. Being intuitive is just another way of saying that you integrate material from a variety of sources quickly and that your ultimate synthesis, while of high quality, may not be completely articulated.

There are, of course, some items that you cannot skip. You always need to consult with your supervisor even if s/he has delegated all international matters to you and does not keep current on the regulatory issues. You may have to give him/her the facts and background information and propose a decision that you think is sound. S/He may come to another conclusion; you do not always have to agree with him/her, but you always need to make sure that you are not making decisions that contradict established institutional policy or clearly articulated law or regulation.

Regardless of whether you arrive at decisions quickly or more slowly, understanding the overall process and being intentional about your own path are important. Let's examine the steps:

1. *Gathering the facts.* What are the facts? List them. Experiment with diagramming the problem—you may be quite surprised at what this yields. Who are the players? What are the desired outcomes? Who has the power in the situation? What's within your discretion and what is decided outside your sphere of influence? Is the case in front of you unique? Or does it represent an entire class of problems? Is this problem worth the time and energy it will take you to sort it out?
2. *Research.* Is there already institutional policy on this question? What does your boss say? What does the NAFSA manual say? Does it refer you to any sections in immigration law or regulation? If so, read the actual regulations. Don't count on someone else to do this for you. Make the leap to being an independent reader. Investigate sources other than the NAFSA manual—has anyone done any legal work on this topic? Consult experienced advisers at institutions similar to yours (location, private, public, small, large, technical, religious, etc.) and ask them if they have answers or opinions.
3. *Set up a thesis.* Then pose the opposite, the antithesis. Create a T diagram with all the arguments in the appropriate column. Are there overlaps? Is there clear guidance and/or regulation that pushes you in one direction or another? Sort out which items have outside authority and which items are your own personal convictions. What is appropriate in this case? Do you understand the difference?
4. *Discuss your ideas with your supervisor.* S/he needs to make a similar decision about whether or not to send the issue up the ladder. This will give you time to think about all the parts of the discussion. Given a few days, one idea may look more important or compelling than the others.
5. *Complete the process by arriving at a synthesis of all these ideas.* In consultation with your supervisor and your colleagues, articulate your decision. While good decisionmaking is not always linear or sequential, implementation and communication of a policy like this must be linear and sequential. Once you move into an arena where your actions affect others, you have an ethical obligation to be clear in your decision. **If you cannot clearly articulate your decision, you are not ready to go public with it.**
6. *Implement your decision.*

CASE STUDY **Undocumented Student** *(Adviser Grapples with the Gray Areas)*

A staff member in the admissions office comes to you with a question about an applicant, Mel Good. All the staff member knows is that Mel is not in lawful "immigration status." You can't ascertain if Mel entered the United States without inspection (i.e., is undocumented), if he started out being in status and overstayed, or if he violated a rule that renders him out of status. Can your campus enroll Mel anyway?

This question arises on virtually every campus in a bewildering variety of forms. It involves immigration law, institutional policy, distinctions between types of institutions, an examination of personal beliefs, and attention to political climate. Given this tough problem, let's examine how we might solve it.

Consider these ideas:

➜ There is nothing in immigration law or regulations that says that colleges and universities must inquire about immigration status in the application process. (There *are* specific regulations stating that a person in B status cannot be enrolled in full-time study. Compliance with this regulation is the responsibility of the individual.)

➜ If the law is silent on a topic, you and your university are free to make policy that makes sense for your own particular institution. If your institution is part of a larger system (e.g., the University of Texas system), you are now ready to begin consultation with other campuses in your system. If your institution is small and independent, you are now ready to begin consultation at the campus level.

And, as hard as it may be for some people to accept this legal principle, it is one of the fundamental concepts in understanding decisionmaking and the proper exercise of discretion:

UNLESS IT IS PROHIBITED, IT IS PERMITTED.

Where can you get help in developing this kind of problem-solving, decisionmaking, ethical balancing, and exercise of discretion? An excellent place to start is consultation with your supervisor and your colleagues at other institutions. One way of interacting with colleagues at other institutions is through e-mail exchanges. These sometimes begin with a general question posed to a wide audience and then a follow-up discussion between two individuals.

E-mail Exchanges on Admission of Undocumented Student

Consider the following exchange (adapted from an actual series of e-mails between one of the authors and a colleague at another institution), keeping the following general questions in mind as you read: Do the arguments seem convincing? Do they square with your own research? Can you sort out an argument from authority from an argument that has its own internal logic? Are these things mutually exclusive?

Dear Colleagues,

I'm trying to initiate discussion with our senior-level administrators regarding international student enrollment policies. In preparation, I am doing some research about the policies of other private institutions in our area.

Can you tell me what your policy is with regard to enrolling students who are out of status and/or are undocumented aliens? Was this policy solely established by the international student office or was it established with the input of senior-level staff (i.e., provost's office, president's office, general counsel)?

I am trying to clarify my institution's policies and wanted to be able to provide examples of what other private institutions are doing. Any information you can provide would be greatly appreciated.

Thank you.

Signed,

A. New Adviser

Dear New Adviser,

My understanding is that my institution does everything in its power to encourage promising applicants to get into appropriate status. But would we deny admission and an I-20 to a student who is otherwise undocumented? No. Would we make a careful determination as to whether it would be safe for the student to exit the U.S.? Yes, we would. If we think that the student would be in danger of the three- or ten-year bar (if you don't know what this is, check your *NAFSA Adviser's Manual)*, we would refer the student to an immigration attorney. We don't make that determination, but we urge the student to get a definitive answer from a qualified immigration attorney. But in the end, would we deny admission solely on the basis of the student being undocumented? NO. Admission is an academic decision.

But would we ever employ an undocumented student? NO. To be practical, few could afford to come to my institution without a teaching or research assistantship. So, it isn't likely to happen often here since we are ungodly expensive. Virtually all our graduate students have either teaching or research assistantships. That's the I-9 part.

The admissions situation is somewhat different for offices that operate as a function of the state. (The employment/assistantship questions are the same for everyone.) State institutions are more constrained in the amount of discretion they can exercise, and they should consult with their counsel and university policy regarding enrolling undocumented students. You can imagine that there are all kinds of access issues for people whose parents have paid state taxes for years despite the fact that one or the other of the parents (and/or the student) may or may not be documented. It's a sticky set of questions with (I would bet) conflicting law. Private institutions are, of course, not bound by what goes on in the tax-supported systems, but it might be worth a look to see what they do.

Signed,

An Old Adviser

Dear Old Adviser,

Thank you for your thoughtful response. In the event that a student at your institution falls out of status after already starting school, do you permit the student to continue as a full-time student (say, if the student didn't want to apply for reinstatement or didn't want to reenter to regain status)?

Signed,

A New Adviser

Dear New Adviser,

If the student has a legitimate (per the regulations) excuse for being out of status that he/she has cleared with the adviser, we can indicate this to DHS in SEVIS. People make all kinds of decisions about their relationship with DHS, but we never tell DHS that they are in status when they are not. It's never an option to tell the government something that isn't true.

But if the student wants to remain in the United States without status, that's his/her choice. We aren't scanning for students who are out of status—they may have been so for years and, if they apply to our school as domestic students, we'd have no way of knowing that they are out of status. It's none of our business. Their academic standing is un-coupled from their immigration status.

Again, the student has the relationship with DHS; you as a representative of your institution have a different relationship that does not include barring the student from attending your institution as a result of problems with DHS. Not an easy concept! But it's at the heart of understanding that advisers never use a person's immigration status as a reason for kicking a student out of school.

Signed,

An Old Adviser

Dear Old Adviser,

Thanks for the additional insight. The information you've provided me has been very helpful in elucidating the distinction between adviser/educator and immigration enforcer.

Do you think the government is going to make that distinction less clear? Since schools are required to monitor student status and report to DHS via SEVIS, do you think the government considers schools more liable for enrolling out-of-status students? Would the government view it as irresponsible and therefore use that against a school when applying for recertification? From my understanding, schools are permitted to enroll students who are out of status, but do you think SEVIS and the move of SEVIS to the U.S. ICE bureau is going to make this less permissible?

Signed,

A New Adviser

Dear New Adviser,

I have some thoughts on the very good questions you're posing. I'll probably sound a little strong on these opinions, but I've been in the field for a very long time and have had time to develop some thoughts. First, the feds don't care at all about your job and how you feel about your job and how you see your role. They care about "security." Not to defend DHS but they are only carrying out a congressional mandate. As individuals, these folks may or may not want to enforce SEVIS but they have no choice since that's what Congress (and presumably the American people) asked them to do.

The artful and moral construction of your job is your task, not theirs. All this reporting has been on the books for a couple of decades—as long as I've been in the field. The INS (pre-Department of Homeland Security) didn't enforce the rules but they were there. So, the moral dilemma is no different now than it was 20 years ago. It's just that we're doing the reporting electronically and more efficiently now. But the moral question remains the same: am I an extension of the government or am I an advocate for the students? The answer is neither and both. It's your mix. The NAFSA Code of Ethics is crystal clear on this concept: an ethical adviser never uses a student's immigration situation as a basis for making academic or personal decisions or to force the student's hand in a particular set of circumstances.

We have two forces at work: the regulations and our role as advocates and advisers. We need to stay in compliance with the regulations. Do they say that a school cannot enroll an out-of-status student? No. They are silent on this matter, for a variety of very good reasons. There is competing law: a public institution can't discriminate on the basis of alienage. Does that apply to international students? Maybe. Maybe not. But schools shouldn't base academic decisions on immigration status because we cannot possibly know what lies behind a student's decision to be out of status. Carelessness? Ignorance? Parental inattention? Compelling family situations? Conditions in one's home country?

Would DHS decide to make a negative finding on recertification if your school enrolled an out-of-status student? They'd have a hard time making a case since there's nothing in the regulations that tells you that you have to ask a student anything about his/her status. Would they know? Maybe. But, are you a party to the relationship between the student and DHS? The CLEAR answer to that question is no.

Do I think that the political climate in the United States is terrible for international students right now? Yes, I do. Should we give up in the face of that? No. We need to be meticulous about our SEVIS reporting, extraordinarily careful in our immigration advising and really energetic in our counseling relationship with these students.

Signed,

A Very Old Adviser

Dear Very Old Adviser,

Thanks so much for your thoughts on this issue. I appreciate your strong opinions because they are rooted in experience and practice. I really appreciate you taking the time to have this dialogue with me because when I started in my job last April, I was brand new to this field and did not have a frame of reference with which to operate (the previous adviser had already departed four months prior to my arrival). As the international student adviser, I'm pretty much it when it comes to all things international and immigration, so sometimes it's hard for me to start the discussions here because most just dismiss these issues. Currently, my institution accepts students regardless of immigration status, but unfortunately does not permit out-of-status students to enroll. Nine months, two NAFSA conferences, numerous conversations with others in the field, and thousands of listserv e-mails later, I want to revisit this policy and open it up to further discussion. To make a long story short, thanks for your time because the information you have provided me will strengthen my reasons for wanting to amend our policy.

Signed,

A Not Completely New Adviser

The letters from "Old Adviser" help to separate the legal issues from the ethical issues and make clear how "New Adviser" can map out a plan of action based on how s/he now understands her/his legal obligations and ethical obligations. As you read through this exchange, go back to the analytical questions. Did you find yourself swinging from one side to the other on the issues? Could you sort out whether you were responding from an ethical consideration or a regulatory consideration or a moral consideration? Other practitioners have examined this issue in some detail and written it up in a way that will give you some guidance in formulating your own position (Badger and Yale-Loehr 2002). Doing this kind of research is part of the formation of your own synthesis and refining your own stand. It is not always tidy, but it is the compelling nature of being a professional.

CASE STUDY

Student Bitten by the Love Bug
(Adviser Bitten by Too-Much-Information Bug)

You work closely with a small group of international students and American students on International Week. You form fast friendships with this group since they are of enormous help and make significant contributions to your programming efforts. It is easy to see couples forming between members of the committee. A few months after your wildly successful International Week, one couple (an international and an American) makes an appointment to come and see you in your office. They arrive, shyly holding hands. They want to talk about getting married. They have all kinds of questions: what kinds of problems do cross-cultural couples face? How will their families deal with the fact that they will be living far from home? You have some expertise in this field and are happy to discuss these interesting topics. But the final question is (as with most counseling sessions) the one they really came for. They want you to help them with the green card part of this big step they are thinking of taking. What do you do?

Consider the following questions:

- Isn't immigration advising for international students an integral part of your job?
- Is this part of immigration in your job description?
- What could happen to the students if you give bad advice?
- What could happen to you if you give bad advice?
- What could happen to your institution if you give bad advice?

Some of the answers lie in the boundaries of your job description, some in an understanding of the structures in the law and regulation, and some in a firm grasp of ethical conduct. This is one of the many times that a solid understanding of the overall picture will really help you solve the problem that is right in front of you.

Read the discussion in Appendix C of the concept called "unauthorized practice of law." Take another look at the NAFSA Code of Ethics in Appendix B. Discuss the case with your supervisor. Collect information. Did your final decision on what to do change?

One good outcome of thinking about these types of issues before the students are sitting in the international office is that you can learn to pace your advising differently. People who take jobs like international advising often are people who seek to solve problems. We are accustomed to being the source of accurate immigration information for the international population on our campuses. But faced with a problem like this one, we need to rethink the paradigm. We need to go through the analytic process because we are in what we now recognize as a different landscape.

There is a great deal of gray is these discussions. It's clear that we should not offer advice in our capacity as international advisers merely as a favor to a friend. It is also clear that we must recognize our own limitations. This is where the discussion about competence and ethical conduct again comes to the fore. It is true that a little knowledge is a dangerous thing. Half-baked advice can easily hurt the very people we intend to help. Recall that the ethical principle to do no harm overrides the principle of benefiting others. It is unethical to raise someone's hopes if you know you are not able (because of your skills or your position) to provide the service they need.

You also need to be cautious in providing legal advice in other areas where students or scholars encounter problems. Two of the most common legal issues students and scholars have to deal with are traffic violations and landlord/tenant disputes, especially lease and deposit terms. Again, refer students to appropriate legal help. It is best to give a list of resources and encourage students to contact several of them before making any decisions. It is not considered ethically sound practice to refer students to only one source of help since that may be construed as an endorsement of that attorney's work.

Any responsible international adviser refers personal legal matters to competent counsel. A common refrain for international advisers is, "I don't do taxes. I don't do marriages. I don't do divorces. I don't do appendectomies or brain surgery. I don't practice law or medicine without a license."

How Professionals Create a Good Supervisory Environment for Themselves

Few international advisers work in an environment in which they are completely unsupervised. At the same time, supervisors in higher education units generally have not had much training in how to supervise and evaluate others. Based on our own experiences, over the course of your career you can expect to have some excellent supervisors, some not so great ones, and even some nonexistent or terrible ones. These differences may be due to personality, organizational structure, or other factors, but no matter what kind of supervision you have, it will definitely affect the future direction of your career path. Therefore, strange as this may seem, one of the more subtle forms of self-regulation you might want for yourself as a professional is to establish a mutually agreeable process for supervision and evaluation with your supervisor. This is a delicate matter, but interpersonal skill is supposed to be a strength of international advisers, so you can do this. Our many years of experience with a variety of bosses have led us to create a short list of tips you might want to consider for successful interactions with your supervisor:

- Building trust with your boss is a two-way street; give her/him plenty of reasons to trust you.
- If you can make your boss look good, it reflects favorably on you; if you make sure that your boss actually *does* good (works), that's even better.

- Keep your boss apprised of any troubling questions or problems you are dealing with. S/He may enjoy surprises of the birthday party-type, but not surprises of the angry dean-type.
- Have regularly scheduled appointments with your boss.
- Ask your boss for advice and counsel.
- Ask your boss how s/he likes to have information delivered: face-to-face, e-mail, phone, etc.
- Learn your boss's work style and personal preferences: informal conversations in the hall, structured meetings with staff, one-on-ones in her/his office, no talking until after s/he's had coffee, etc.

Having a positive work relationship with your boss sets the stage for being able to discuss complex situations and ethical issues in a collegial manner without each case becoming a "problem" for which you need counsel. This approach is less stressful for both of you and creates an environment that makes it easier to deal with truly problematic situations when they do come up. One issue for which you most certainly need your boss's support is if you experience workplace discrimination. International advisers sometimes face discrimination based on a number of factors. Sometimes students are not happy to find their adviser is an immigrant, especially if the adviser comes from a country that has a problematic history with the students' country. Male students and scholars are sometimes unaccustomed to dealing with women in positions of authority. By having a good supervisory relationship with your boss, s/he should know the quality of your work and stand behind you in such situations. That's what good bosses do when they have good employees.

FOLLOW-UP ACTIVITIES

1. Go to the NAFSA Code of Ethics in Appendix B and read it carefully.
2. Talk to your boss about the supervision and evaluation issues raised in this chapter.
3. Identify a mentor (your own personal "Old Adviser") and/or a group of colleagues with whom you can discuss the complicated cases outlined in this chapter.
4. Spend some time reading the actual immigration regulations, not just the *NAFSA Adviser's Manual* so that you get a sense of how they differ.
5. Write out in detail some complex cases you have dealt with. Identify the legal and ethical issues, and go through the processes outlined in this chapter for developing sound responses.

Works Cited and Resources

Althen, Gary. 1995. *The Handbook of Foreign Student Advising, Revised Edition*. Intercultural Press, Inc., p. 197–198.

Badger, Ellen, and Stephen Yale-Loehr. 2002. "They Can't Go Home Again: Undocumented Aliens and Access to U.S. Higher Education." http://www.twmlaw.com/resources/general-42cont.htm (accessed November 2005).

Dessoff, Alan. 2006. "A Key to Your Career." *International Educator*, Vol. 15, No. 1, p. 36–43.

Kegan, Robert. 1994. *In Over Our Heads: The Mental Demands of Modern Life*. Cambridge, MA: Harvard University Press.

Kitchener, Karen. S. 1984. "Intuition, Critical Evaluation and Ethical Principles: The Foundation for Ethical Decisions in Counseling Psychology." *The Counseling Psychologist*, Vol. 12, p. 43–55.

Kitchener, Karen. S. 2000. *Foundations of Ethical Practice, Research, and Teaching in Psychology*. Mahwah, NJ: Lawrence Erlbaum Associates.

Pemberton, J. Michael. 1991. "If Being a CRM is the Answer, What is the Question?" *Records Management Quarterly*, Vol. 25. p. 50–53.

Pemberton, J. Michael. 1992. "ARMA (Association of Records Managers and Administrators) International's Code of Professional Responsibility." *Records Management Quarterly*, Vol. 26, p. 42–45.

Rosser, Vicki J., Jill M. Hermsen, Ketevan Mamiseishvili, and Melinda S. Wood. Forthcoming January 2007. "The Impact of SEVIS on U.S. International Student and Scholar Advisors." Higher Education: *The International Journal of Higher Education and Planning*. Dordrecht: Springer Netherlands.

TAKING THE NEXT STEPS ON YOUR CAREER PATH

CHAPTER 6

By now, you probably have set in motion quite a few changes aimed toward improving the environment for international students and scholars on your campus. We hope you have honed your interpersonal skills and problem-prevention tactics along the way. So this is a good time to reflect on your work thus far and to think ahead a bit. Go back and ask yourself the question from Chapter 1, "How do you envision your career ten years from now?" Just as you have developed your skills in planning and advocacy for the students and scholars you serve, you need to think strategically about your career and the path you want to follow. Some people think that being a strategic thinker means being calculating. We disagree. Think of it more like the Boy Scout motto, "be prepared." If you want to reach a specific place on your career path, you need to have a plan for getting there. This chapter will help to identify some key tools that may help you move along that path.

Long-Term Planning

You are going to create your own path/route based on your values, interests, and talents. Whatever your decisions, they are legitimate choices that you make in the broader context of your life. You will, of course, encounter people who think you should have taken another path or tapped area different set of your skills and talents. Even though this book lays out a number of options for paths for you to consider, we certainly do not value one over another.

Mindsets

In Chapter 1 we suggested a number of instruments that could help you identify work-related interests and personal characteristics that fit with various kinds of occupations. We believe there are a number of additional predispositions, characteristics, or traits that effective international advisers share. For lack of a better term, we refer to them as mindsets. This term implies that they are something you are conscious of and something you can cultivate with practice.

Curiosity

Do you come to work wondering what new and maybe surprising thing is going to turn up that day? Do you like, rather than dread, the unexpected? When you have a peculiar or awkward interaction with someone, do you wonder about what made the situation strange or do you shrug it off?

Analytical Approach to Problem Solving

In the case of the strange interaction, do you try to think of several explanations that all make sense or could be plausible? Do you turn to a cross-cultural reference for insight? As you develop your expertise in immigration regulations, do you rely only on your NAFSA *Adviser's Manual* as your bible or do you also turn to the Code of Federal Regulations as well as some legal references? Then do you meet with colleagues and enjoy a thoughtful conversation about ambiguous regulatory language, the intent of the regulations, and various interpretations and practices among international advisers?

Willingness to Experiment

When you get stuck on one of the SEVIS data input screens, how do you react—do you try hitting several links just to see what happens, or simply logout in frustration rather than possibly making a mistake on a student record? Do you think your school's international dinner event has become too predictable so you want to try a whole new approach to showcasing food from various countries? What is your level of tolerance for risk or uncertainty in various situations?

Taking the Perspective of Others

This is a vital cross-cultural competency. International advisers tend to be pretty good at doing this in a cultural setting and less practiced at doing it in other contexts. For example, as noted in Chapter 2, when an irate faculty member chews you out, can you take his or her perspective in which faculty are the center of the academic universe and we all are here solely to help them meet their scholarly objectives (which is actually pretty accurate but they don't need to be rude about reminding us)?

Metacognition/Mindfulness/Intentionality

Are you consciously aware of your thought processes? Do you realize when you have exceeded the limits of your knowledge and when you need to learn more before you make a decision? In psychology this is called metacognition—thinking about thinking. There is research that suggests people with limited knowledge of a subject *over*estimate what they know while those with much more knowledge tend to *under*estimate their expertise (Kruger and Dunning 1999). This argument implies that people who are real experts are not faking modesty about their achievements ("no, really, I couldn't have earned this Nobel Prize without my wonderful creative colleagues"), but it also lends credence to the adage that "a little knowledge is a dangerous thing." A slightly different way of thinking of this is as "mindfulness"—a concept found in many spiritual and religious traditions—characterized by deliberation or perhaps choosing not to act when your first reaction is to jump in and do something. This trait is not part of the American ethos of "act now, ask questions later," nor does it come easily to new professionals wanting to demonstrate that they can do the job.

These traits can be integrated into a mindset that willingly engages in the complexity of ideas and the ambiguity of situations. In much of the work of international advising, speed is not a goal. Of course you need to meet deadlines, but you also need to be a detective who observes and listens carefully, looks for subtle points that could be glossed over by a less astute adviser, and then deliberates about the implications of various outcomes rather than coming to an easy conclusion that might close off other options prematurely. A mindset that enables you to enjoy the multifaceted nature of the processes, not just the outcomes, of your interactions with students and scholars will serve you well during your career.

Skill Sets

In addition to gauging how well these mindsets fit with the mental characteristics you bring to your career, there are a number of general skill sets you should develop to be effective and advance in international advising. A closer look at these concerns (and your interest and/or disinterest in them) may do more to frame your long-term plans than some grandiose 20-year scheme. Unlike many of the specific skills we have addressed in previous chapters, the ones listed here are generalizable across many professions and work in various higher education settings, not just international advising.

Negotiating or Defining Your Role

It is important to understand the functions of your position and your office and to weigh them against how you and your office are perceived by others. On some campuses, there is a pervasive attitude that if a question has anything to do with anything international or if the problem involves anyone from another country, it is yours to solve. This might take the form of a cranky call from the Payroll office demanding that *you* deal with the equally cranky international scholar who cannot understand why he has to pay Social Security taxes when he is never going to retire in the United States. It might take the form of a polite but insistent call from an American professor asking about how to get a visa to go to Iceland (after all, you *are* the visa office, aren't you?). Or, it might take the form of an administrator who expects you to edit a survey instrument with an eye toward how the "internationals" might read it.

You may or may not respond to any or all of these demands. It is up to you to negotiate with your boss to define your role in serving international students and scholars at your campus. In some situations, you may respond because you genuinely feel that the request is within the purview of your role; in others, you respond because it is politically wise to do so; and in still others, you respond because you need to build bridges for future collaborative efforts. How your role is defined may change over time, so it's helpful to periodically review this matter with your boss as your skills develop.

Setting Boundaries

The matter of role definition is closely tied to the scope of your position and the delicate skill of boundary setting. This will help you in establishing appropriate limits on your time and energy. Is your office seen as a dumping ground, a haven, a resource, a counseling center, a programs office, or maybe as an extension of the Department of Homeland Security? If you don't know the parameters of your position, then don't expect other people to be able to guess whether a particular task or question is appropriate or inappropriate for you. Gary Althen (1995) offered an excellent analysis of these paradigms. Some of the boundaries will probably be set by your institutional leadership, the campus culture, or office tradition so you may need to adjust your personal expectations for boundaries as a new employee. In any case, it is worth your time to discuss boundary setting with your boss (and perhaps office mates). A clear understanding of what you and your office do and (more importantly) *do not* do should be established within the office and then communicated gently but firmly to those you serve and to other parts of the campus.

Acknowledging these limits and integrating them into your work style can be an even bigger challenge, given the level of commitment many international advisers have for their work. Heartfelt passion for your work can lead to the dubious assumption that you can never have uninterrupted time because there may be a student who needs help, and not just any help—*your* help. In some ways, this is a tyranny to which many student services professionals fall prey. International advisers often feel an additional burden because of the federally mandated immigration function that is part of the job. Of course it falls upon your shoulders to advise students properly about immigration matters, but if DHS employees can take time off, international advisers most certainly can.

Time Management

Once some mutually agreeable boundaries on your work are set, managing your work time becomes easier. As the speed of technology and the access to multiple means of communication have increased, so has the pace of daily work. Even in higher education, with its painfully slow processes of shared governance and decisionmaking, there is a tendency to value speed and productivity, and international advisers certainly feel this pressure to develop systems of efficiency through online advising, Web-based communication, and batch processing with SEVIS.

Based on what we have said previously about the nature of professionalism, we believe that serving students and scholars in an ethical manner requires international advisers to spend time on research and deliberation—learning and thinking. The learning part, for example, includes meeting the individuals with whom you had ten e-mail exchanges about the requirements for practical training. Electronic communication is not as sensitive as face-to-face interaction, and it sometimes isn't as efficient as it's touted to be. Nearly everyone has experienced how a simple typo in an e-mail can lead to a miscommunication that requires numerous time consuming messages to clear up. By the same token, cranking out 50 immigration forms in one morning is not efficient if 5 of them contain errors that derail the academic plans of the people who will use them. We cannot stress enough that *accuracy* trumps *timeliness* when it comes to immigration paperwork.

So, here is a critical time-management skill for all international advisers:

CLOSE YOUR DOOR ONCE IN A WHILE.

It doesn't mean to slam the door in your supervisor's face. In fact, some directors insist on an open door policy. If that's the policy in your office, you should still try to rationalize to your supervisor why you need a certain amount of time when you do *not* see students. Experienced advisers often find that a combination of scheduled appointments, open walk-in times, and no appointments allowed time (closed door) works best. This ensures you will have uninterrupted time to research sticky problems, plan ahead for needed professional development, or consult with other experts. Overall, this is likely to improve your day-to-day operations and your mental health.

Technology Skills

Until about 2001, technology skills would not have been a requirement in any job description for an international adviser position. This is clearly no longer the case. The efficient use of technology affects your time-management skills as much as it affects your direct use of technology for things such as SEVIS reporting. Because most computer users these days are self-taught, the range of skills that any one person may have is quite idiosyncratic. We are always amazed at colleagues who don't know how to do a particular function in word processing (e.g., inserting a particular kind of graphic, something we thought "anyone" could do), but they are experts at Web design (an area in which we still struggle).

Some international offices have coped with rapidly changing technology needs by hiring a tech specialist. In some situations, this person is a SEVIS data entry and maintenance person, and in others, they maintain the office Web site or other technology-based services. Not every office can support a separate position for technology needs so you may be expected to have a wide range of computer skills. We assume that because new advisers have grown up using computers they will have much more experience with a variety of applications compared with some of their senior colleagues (who probably have quite a variety of computer skills but they may not be as comprehensive). Though it can change very quickly, if you want or need to be the "go to" person in your office, we offer the following list of functions in which you should have at least a fair level of competence. They can help you to achieve good time management and a modicum of sanity in your demanding job.

- Relatively complex word processing skills
- Functional ability to create or modify spread sheets (e.g., Microsoft Excel®)[1]
- Basic understanding of how to use database programs (such as FSAtlas®) to extract data and write reports
- Basic understanding of database systems that are used on your campus as the official "databases of record" (such as PeopleSoft® or Banner®), including how these systems interact with each other. This is usually campus-based knowledge that you have to learn on the job.
- Task and calendar management systems
- Mass mailing (snail- and e-mail) software, e.g. how to do a mail merge
- Basic understanding of presentation and graphics software

As a subset of these technical skills, we recommend some pertinent "soft" skills that can enable you to use the technology more effectively.

- Awareness of how graphic layout and presentation of content may be perceived by a non-U.S. audience (e.g., knowing what kind of photos should be avoided in recruiting materials. For example, most international advisers know to avoid the American "thumbs up" or "A-OK" gestures on published materials because those gestures have very different meanings in some other cultures. It's not only gestures, but clothing that matters as well. What is appropriately "casual" dress for an American audience might be viewed as immodest elsewhere.)
- Willingness to interact constructively with the evolving SEVIS data tracking system for international students and scholars developed by the Department of Homeland Security (e.g., participating in online training opportunities, sharing "work around" solutions with colleagues, etc).

Your office and campus may require you to utilize specific business process packages (e.g., Windows Office XP®, Banner®, an in-house UNIX system, etc.). Our experience suggests that younger professionals have less trouble changing from one software type/brand to another, but if you are not very flexible, you should probably start learning some of the new packages now rather than when under pressure. Or if you are very persuasive, you may be able to create a system or convince your boss to buy one of the packages currently on the market; but don't count on this option.

[1] Listing of commercial products is not to be construed as an endorsement of the product, but merely to serve as examples where generic terms may not be meaningful to some readers.

In addition to improving your time-management skills, understanding technology is one of the keys to gaining a "place at the table" in campus-wide discussions. One of the positive outcomes of SEVIS implementation was a new level of interaction between international offices and the Registrar on the F-1 side and Human Resources on the J-1 side. Because SEVIS implementation had a sense of urgency in the months following September 11, it was suddenly easier for international offices to get the attention and money they needed for software and cooperation.

Cross-Cultural Skills

Like many others, you may have come to the profession of international advising because you had a life-changing, cross-cultural experience and now find yourself interested in a cross-cultural work environment. You may also believe that there are greater benefits to cross-cultural work than the simple human fascination with the world outside your own culture. Whatever your particular background, you may feel that you have a working set of cross-cultural skills. These may include:

- Ability to communicate across linguistic and cultural differences
- Willingness to engage in conversations where the other person is moving into English for the first time
- Careful cultivation of your own English to remove hard-to-understand idioms, slang, contractions, acronyms, etc.
- Sensitivity to the subtle differences of gesture, "body language," and status indicators
- Understanding of basic concepts such as "group-affiliated" versus "individualistic" cultures
- Understanding of what people mean when they talk about "culture shock" and "reverse culture shock"

By whatever means you developed these skills, you may want to enhance your skill base by reviewing the literature on cross-cultural theories, as well as culture-specific literature. We cannot begin to recap this subject adequately in just a few pages, so we strongly recommend you review the resources listed at the end of this chapter. There are a multitude of excellent books, journals, scholarly research, and other works in cross-cultural skills and competency (see #1, Follow-Up Activities, for examples).

Another option is to audit a few cultural anthropology courses on your campus. Although you may think that you are not very interested in theory, the theoretical vocabulary will allow you to frame your own experiences more broadly and to enhance your professional capacity to understand cultural differences. It can be tempting to let your personal experience stand as a proxy for a more formal understanding of cross-cultural issues. Your unique experience is a great starting place for cross-cultural awareness and knowledge, but it should not be the final destination for a "professional" international educator. There is more to working in the field than knowing another language and understanding the "W" curve in cultural adaptation discussions.

The following scenario is a sample case where cross-cultural issues come into play. Read and discuss it with colleagues, and use it as a model for other discussions based on your own international office experiences.

CASE STUDY **The Green Card Dilemma**

You are working on the H-1B petition for Dr. Smirnoff, a new visiting researcher to your campus. In the course of getting the paperwork in place, you've had a nice conversation with the host faculty who lets you know that he hopes that Dr. Smirnoff will be a long-term hire and that a green card is in the picture. Dr. Smirnoff is one of the premier researchers in his field, having more than 25 years of experience and accomplishment. You send Dr. Smirnoff your standard intake form. He returns it only partially completed. You exchange e-mails to get the balance of the information, with the thought that you'll want as much information as possible so you can start planning the strategy for his green card.

In the course of getting the H visas, Dr. Smirnoff experiences some security clearance delays, but they aren't unusual for his profile. He grumbles a bit to his host faculty who gives you a call to clarify. Dr. Smirnoff does not contact you with these questions.

Dr. Smirnoff arrives on campus but doesn't come to orientation. You follow up with a couple of e-mails and finally just send him the information in writing, so you're sure he understands what he needs to travel.

Eight months later the host faculty contacts you with the good news that the research is going well and he'd like to begin the green card process. You invite Dr. Smirnoff to your office to discuss the case. He misses the first appointment but makes the second. The conversation is short, but you finally gather enough information to begin the case, with the help of the department chair, the host faculty, and the department secretary.

The I-140 is easily approved and you ask Dr. Smirnoff to come in to discuss the next steps. Again, he hesitates. In the course of the I-485 discussion, you note that he offers no information. You provide the appropriate level of general information, advising him that he can either do the I-485 himself or hire an attorney. He is polite but noncommittal.

USCIS takes its usual long, long time to adjudicate. Occasionally, you get a call from the host faculty asking why things are taking so long. Dr. Smirnoff continues to be pretty non-communicative. Since you've gone to great lengths to make this process as painless as possible, you're at a loss as to why this case hasn't resulted in the usual happy relationship with the individual.

What's going on in this scenario? What are the core elements of cross-cultural (mis)communication you can identify in your interactions with Dr. Smirnoff? To what extent might age, gender, and nationality play a role in the situation (both his and yours)? In retrospect, what could you have done differently? How would that have changed the interaction? Would it matter? What unanticipated benefits could come out of this apparently frustrating and enigmatic scenario? Where do you draw the line between cultural factors and individual personality?

Program Development and Activities

As with cross-cultural skill building, there is a plethora of information on student programming and activities. Rather than reproduce most of it here, we simply highlight some international programming ideas that many campuses have used. For more information, we recommend meeting with your student affairs or student services office, and with professional associations such as the National Association of Student Personnel Administrators (NASPA).

One of the core program functions of international advisers is to provide orientation for new students and scholars. Some institutions have very elaborate programs for all incoming students so your international component may be relatively simple. But other campuses do very little to orient newcomers and you may have to add a lot of basic activities for the international population. There are multitudes of programs you can draw upon for creating or enhancing your own orientation. As described in Chapter 3, start with your network of allies and see what is already being done by others on your campus and at similar institutions. Why start from scratch when you can learn from others' best practices?

Many campuses recognize the contributions of their international students and scholars by hosting some type of annual international event such as a fair or dinner. Although the whole campus may want to take credit for these sometimes huge events that often draw large numbers of community members onto the campus, most of the real work of planning and implementing them fall on the international office. If you love programming, this kind of activity will allow you to use your creativity and people skills to the max. Some advisers find that after a few years, though, they run out of fresh ideas and prefer to hand this activity over to newer advisers who can bring the event up to a new standard.

When various campus constituents talk about internationalizing the campus, they may mean any number of things. One of these areas can be in changing the curriculum to include more international perspectives through textbook selection. Others may mean focusing a particular curricular component to coincide with specific campus events such as national day celebrations. Partnerships with faculty can make these types of events much more academically substantive while keeping the fun parts that engage people on a nonacademic level.

A common programming challenge that international advisers almost inevitably face is when flags of various countries are displayed. Flags are powerful symbols of national or cultural identity. Institutional decisions that may not seem important to a particular administrator matter a great deal to students, especially if their flag is omitted when others are on display. This can provide a wonderful opportunity for discussions of history and politics both in and out of class, but it must be managed well to ensure that it is a learning experience for everyone involved. For example, some institutions take their guidance from the U.S. State Department and do not display Taiwan's flag because the United States does not have diplomatic relations with Taiwan. On the other hand, if the institution decides to display Taiwan's flag (in addition to China's) because they have students from Taiwan, the Chinese students may complain that the institution is implying a foreign policy statement. The same applies to flying the Palestinian and Israeli flags. This can become quite a quagmire, so some institutions simply decide not to use national flags routinely or for special events. If your campus displays flags from other countries, you can expect to deal with this issue eventually—we encourage you to make the most of it rather than minimizing the possibility of substantive learning about difficult issues.

Office Relationships

It may be that you are currently in your first professional job, or you may have held a variety of positions before this one. Perhaps you have held clerical and/or entry-level professional positions. You may also have experience in fields outside international education or even outside higher education. Whatever your background, you have at least some experience in dealing with office life and politics. You probably can distinguish a good boss from a bad one, and you can recognize people who contribute to the overall mission of the office and those who don't. You probably can identify bad behavior and good behavior at many levels. The following is a short list of topics for conversation either with your supervisor or colleagues:

- What are the differences between "professional" and support roles?
- What do the terms "exempt" and "nonexempt" employee mean?
- Why do some "professional" positions require a degree when the subject matter of the degree is not specified?
- Why do some people engage in passive-aggressive behaviors at work?
- What can other office staff do about it?
- What contributes to and what harms good morale?

A genuine and open discussion of these topics is a start to building good office relationships. The real art is in consistent and fair treatment of everyone in an office. People who succeed in office life have the following skills:

- Willingness to participate in the solution of all office problems, not just one's own
- Ability to express a respectful approach to all
- Calm, even-handed approach to office "crises"
- Willingness to pull one's own weight
- A sense of humor

While this may seem to be mere common sense, a lack of this skill set often creates more problems than more "substantive" problems do. Taking some time to think about what precipitates bad behavior in an office often yields some surprising insight into fellow workers (or even a new insight about yourself!).

One of the toughest situations you may encounter in your office setting is deciding when it may be time for you to move on. A number of situations may precipitate this decision. Some of them are pretty definitive: your office gets reorganized as part of a larger unit shake up, the boss you adore leaves and you can't work with the new one, or you learn that something unethical or illegal is occurring in your office. A more subtle but perhaps even more tricky challenge is deciding what to do when it is very clear that the boss is going to stay in her/his job until it's time to retire, and there is no way that a junior adviser will ever be groomed to move up. This is great for the boss and lousy if you happen to be the junior adviser. If it involves a male boss and a female subordinate, it could be interpreted as sex discrimination but that's another issue. Regardless, you should always be planning ahead for your next ideal position while maintaining a professional demeanor in your current one.

Are You Cut Out for Management?

Not everyone aspires to direct an international office. Some people actively avoid such opportunities because they enjoy serving students or scholars more than they enjoy dealing with personnel issues or other problems of management. You may be in a situation where circumstances dictate that you will never become a director; conversely, you may become a director of an international office literally overnight with little or no preparation. It is a fundamental consideration as to whether you would like to move into a management or director position. There are a number of things you can do to assess your interest level and/or prepare yourself. Taking a look at the characteristics of people who are successful in management is the place to start. Do you possess some or all of these qualities? Could you some day? Do you want to?

- Good managers are generally focused at long-term planning. Do you routinely find yourself thinking about what might happen if your office followed Plan A as opposed to Plan B? Are you always thinking six months out?
- Good managers are big picture thinkers. Are you fascinated by how the International Office fits into Student Affairs? Can you imagine how things might be if the International Office were located in Academic Affairs? Do you think about big questions like how U.S. visa policy affects the number of international students coming to the United States?
- Good managers are systems thinkers. Do you usually seek to understand the entire system? For example, do you need to understand the relationships between data systems before you are willing to go forward with a change in an office procedure? Or, do you think about how other offices at your institution have solved a particular problem?
- Good managers are empathetic and even handed. Do you find yourself understanding the complaints of the Records office when they voice dissatisfaction with how the International Office enters passport names in the database? Do you genuinely see both sides of the question? Are you a mediator of problems or a polarizing force in the office?
- Good managers understand how the money flows. Do you care? Can you tolerate the budget process?
- Good managers are willing to engage questions at a policy level. Do you find yourself wanting to participate in discussions at a policy level? Can you distinguish between the anecdotal and broad principles in problem solving? Can you tolerate the number of meetings that go into making office-level and institutional-level policy?
- Good managers have great zoom lenses. Can you move easily from a discussion on cultural norms to a discussion on what address to use on the I-765 in a practical training application?
- Good managers can balance the needs of the individual with the needs of the group. Can you consider an ethical problem in the abstract without being dragged down by the tyranny of a phrase like, "If I do this for you, I'll have to do it for everyone?"

One challenge that potential managers dread, but need the skills to manage, is how to deal with workplace conflicts. Think about yourself, your abilities, your interests, and your aptitudes as you read this "management readiness" checklist (Ericksen 2005).

1. How do you handle tensions and conflicts with co-workers in the office? (self-initiating resolution, seeking other perspectives to find resolution or complaining, assigning blame)
2. How do you handle dealing with a "difficult" student? (seek more productive strategies, consult mentor, assign blame, sentence to bureaucratic limbo)

3. How do you deal with a campus policy that you think is "unfair"? (seek clarification, suggest improvements, careful research with others or resist, circumvent, complain)
4. How do you deal with another campus office that is presenting difficulties in doing daily work? (workaround, undermine, confront or forge alliances, offer resources, collaboration)
5. How do you keep a supervisor informed? (complaining or offering alternative resolution strategies, consulting for other perspectives)
6. How does your "zoom lens" function? (individual student vs. "big picture" issues)
7. How do you "frame" issues that involve potential conflict? ("problem" or "challenge"?)
8. Is conflict handled with emotions, rigidity, intellect, flexibility, compromise?

Management isn't for everyone. As you chart your course, think about how often conflict resolution plays a part in being a manager. It can be dynamic and it certainly is a higher order task in terms of helping people do their work. You may not be ready for this role as you read this, but maybe you can envision a time when you will be ready. In the meantime, pay attention to good managers (everyone knows when they have the pleasure of working for a good manager!) and learn by positive example. Alternatively, pay attention to the truly wretched managers with whom you come in contact. You can learn just as much from a negative example as from a positive one.

Dealing with Money Matters

Knowledge is power. Money is power. Therefore, knowledge of money is power. The logic may be flawed but the principle is correct. We realize that finance may be even less appealing to most new advisers than advocacy (see Chapter 4), but people who know even a little bit about institutional finance, budgets, and funding can use it very skillfully to increase their credibility and usefulness. This is because the majority of people on campus understand virtually nothing about budgets and finance beyond their own unit. We have already discussed some of the major money issues in higher education in Chapter 2. This is not a primer on academic fiscal structures. Nonetheless, knowing how money works at your institution is an excellent strategic move in your professional development.

So how do fiscal structures affect an international office? Why should you bother to understand contracts and grants, possibly one of the few areas of federal regulations that is harder to understand than immigration? The following example may be helpful.

CASE STUDY **Dollars And Sense**

Susan is an international adviser at the University of East North Dakota. For the past three years, she has been busy with student immigration advising, cultural programming, and office procedures. Recently her office was asked to take on the immigration work for the growing number of international researchers coming to her university to conduct research. Susan is overwhelmed by this additional work, not just because it means that she needs to "see" more people but because it involves more complex law than she had learned in the past. As the population of international scholars grows, she and her boss realize that they need additional help. But the state legislature is adamant about cutting costs and there simply is no funding for another position. Susan's boss asks her to write a proposal about charging fees to requesting departments for immigration work.

Analysis

Susan, as a strategically savvy international adviser, sees that creativity is needed and she knows that someone in her network of campus allies is bound to know more than she does about the scope of research at her institution. By consulting with others she can determine if the university has reached a critical mass in terms of international research staffing overall, and if so, is it possible within the structure of the relevant federal grants to charge an immigration-processing fee for these individuals. Susan will find that there will be differences from one granting agency to the next, but in general terms, grant funds can be divided up into two "pots" (see Chapter 2 for a more detailed discussion of external grants):

1. Money for the research itself. This includes salaries for the researchers, the necessary chemicals, flasks, trips to various sites, and so on. These are "direct" costs.
2. Money to support the research. Examples include a portion of the heating bill, possibly office supplies, and so on. These are "indirect costs."

Susan needs to conduct an informational interview with the person on campus whose job it is to supervise the grant administrators. That office is usually called the Office of Sponsored Research or the Office of Contracts and Grants. While this may seem impossibly remote from the international office, this information may be a key to Susan's solution. Susan does not need to understand the entirety of grant funding any more than the grants office needs to understand immigration regulations, but she does need to know the general framework to tailor her proposal so that she can get what she needs.

Outcome

Susan takes the time to do some background research and determines that she can advocate for an immigration-paperwork-processing fee that comes under the "indirect cost" umbrella.

She consults with her allies, writes a well-crafted proposal, works it through the campus hierarchy, gets the needed approvals to implement a service fee that research projects can charge to their grants as an indirect cost, and hires another person for her office. She has solved the problem of being under-resourced in her office and is better able to meet the institution's needs. She has helped some worthy people doing meaningful work. She has made her job more interesting. She has solved a big problem for her boss. All good outcomes.

Insights from Senior Navigators

You may be feeling overwhelmed by now. If so, it's time to go for a walk, have some of your favorite calming beverage, and relax for a moment. Remember the advice earlier in this chapter, "It is OK to close your door and take a breather." Indeed, one of the key lessons in maintaining your sanity is to give yourself time to think, reflecting on the path that has brought you to where you are today and contemplating a trajectory for where you want to go. Over the years we have collected insights from colleagues who have found success and pleasure in their careers in international advising and who embody at least some of the mindsets and skill sets we have discussed. Their words of wisdom that we provide below come from internet postings, conference sessions (Hallett et al. 2001, Young et al. 1999), publications (Van de Water 2006), and personal conversations with some of them.

On Managing Time and the Workload

One adviser suggested "Learn to say 'no,' or at least 'This is going to take a while.'. . .Try to manage one's own expectations and those of others." Another commented, "Technology clearly helps us serve our clients more effectively and efficiently, but it is not a time saver. E-mail applies more pressure to staff to work faster and harder. Coping strategies include keeping a sense of humor and a full life outside the office as a means to balancing the craziness that faces us every day." One commented on the benefits of getting out of the office on a regular to basis and taking a walk to review your decisions; it helps you to see if you are making them in a consistent manner.

Ethical Dilemmas

One adviser discussed at length the notions of confidentiality vs. good sense. "The typical American university's confidentiality regulations make perfect sense to most Americans. They share an understanding of and reverence for 'privacy.' They really believe that people operate on their own. People from many other countries don't share these assumptions, of course. Situations arise where keeping things secret from family members almost guarantees that things will get worse. Yet that is what we are expected to do. Sometimes it is necessary to make a difficult decision: should we follow the cultural-based assumptions about individualism and privacy, to the likely detriment of one of our clients, or should we make the situation known to people who might be able to help with it?" (Note: By this time, you are probably tuned into FERPA regulations. If you don't recognize this term, ask your boss. You'll want to take this into consideration when you are operating in this realm.)

With regard to tough ethical issues, a senior adviser said, "The most difficult decisions related to situations in which international students I was advising had bent the truth in order to survive financially, e.g. failing to disclose some support from home in order to gain a scholarship. This left me with the moral quandary of whether to report all the facts to the appropriate office. More and more in my career, I came down on the side of reporting all the verifiable facts in order to maintain the total integrity of my office which I had worked so hard to establish."

Office Politics and Management

In dealing with staff, a senior adviser commented, "If the environment includes judgmental participants, self-righteousness, impatience, or the need to up-stage others, then decisions suffer. If it doesn't, decisions will much more often be right or at least defensible." Another noted, "Figuring out why a staff member is unhappy and whether they are justified in their views when they complain is hard. Encouraging more positive attitudes or helping a person find a more appropriate place of employment—these are difficult tasks. It's a real challenge to figure out how much personal time to grant to people who need extra time for very good reasons. It's an art to know what to do when someone loses his/her temper."

Van de Water (2006) reiterates the important part that faculty play in shaping the role of the international adviser on campus. "Faculty *are* the heart of the academic community.... This is a fundamental reality that is—too often in my experience—not understood or fully appreciated. The successful international education administrator must develop a management philosophy that reflects the central role of the faculty, department heads, and deans." Understanding this perspective, even if you don't agree with it, will help advisers manage their interactions with faculty much more effectively.

Bureaucratic Tangles (Inside and Outside the Institution) and Exercise of Discretion

On dealing with grey areas, one senior adviser said, "Part of the issue has to do with the ability to rank grey areas in immigration law as to whether or not the world will suffer if we stretch to accommodate a client's needs. I don't mean break the law, but when a judgment call arises, do we consistently side with the client or the government? I prefer to try my best to side with the client." With regard to decisions about what type of visa can be used by postdoctoral fellows (a frequently debated issue at many institutions) one adviser commented, "It's very, very tough to shepherd this topic within a complex institutional environment, particularly when dealing with aggressive clients and powerful faculty. Setting a policy and sticking to it is very important."

In response to an e-mail query about work visas, one astute adviser commented "I guess this is another situation in which lack of regulations leads to many reasonable positions on an issue." He then goes on to cite the statute and explain how he came to his conclusion but also suggested, "I recognize that that's not the only valid understanding of the law," leaving the door open for others to develop their own line of reasoning and decisionmaking.

Career Planning in General

As you think about where you would like to go professionally, one office director noted that "peripheral vision is necessary. Don't be so focused on a particular goal that you preclude other choices." He pointed out that activities that seem marginal to your core functions today can become central in the future; we commented on this in the discussion of the increased importance of computers and technology skills.

Bon Voyage!

Through these reflections, it is clear that even the most seasoned among us still need to ponder the difficult questions. None of this is easy and it is seldom routine. You can be fairly certain that as soon as you feel you have pretty good mastery of the F-1 visa regulations, Congress will enact changes that require you to learn a whole new set of vaguely defined terms and conditions pertaining to international students and scholars. It is complex work, there are many variables and influences, and it all happens in a profoundly cross-cultural environment without enough time for the necessary thoughtful analysis.

But in the long run, this career allows us to aid in the overall goal of increasing the exchange of new ideas and knowledge across national borders by improving the international mobility of individuals. In this process, we get to know some of the smartest, most interesting and risk-taking students and scholars in the world. You will probably someday be able to say, "I remember when Rongyin was a just another nervous undergraduate here; I can't believe she's now a Nobel Laureate in Physics," or "I remember persuading Costas to sing for our international student reception and now he's singing at the Metropolitan Opera," or even, "Antonella was such a cut-up when she was here, it's hard to imagine her as the Minister of Education in Peru now." Sometimes it is hard to keep the big picture in mind as we deal with each person that comes through our office door, but as we build our collection of success stories one by one, it becomes clear that this is work in which the rewards outweigh the challenges for the most part. Maybe that's what kept the very capable senior advisers we've cited in the field for so long.

And maybe it is at least part of what is motivating you to start your career in this field. As you find the path that is best for you to follow as an international educator, we hope you find the navigational tools we have provided to be helpful. We also hope that you will discover new tools that will help to shape the profession as it evolves. We wish you the best on the extraordinary journey ahead!

FOLLOW-UP ACTIVITIES

1. Start to build your intercultural resource library. One good start is the Intercultural Press (www.interculturalpress.com/). Other sources are:

   Culture Matters. Peace Corps training manual/workbook, available online at www.peacecorps.gov/wws/culturematters

   Journal of Intercultural Communication Research, published by Routledge

   International Journal of Intercultural Relations, published by Elsevier

   Please note that this list is by no means comprehensive nor do we endorse these sources over any others; it is just a sample.
2. Read some books on time management and office politics such as *Getting to Yes: Negotiating Agreement without Giving In*, by Fisher, Ury, and Patton (1991).
3. Get to know the person on your campus who heads up the office that administers contracts and grants. Conduct an "informational interview." Ask for background material. Ask for a pie chart of the principal sources of grant funding on your campus.
4. Identify objects or activities that help you maintain constructive mindsets at work: your favorite kind of tea to drink when you get stressed or busy, plants on your desk that put oxygen back into the air, an electronic or paper calendar on which you can make an appointment with yourself for quiet time, comfortable shoes under your desk for times when you need to go out for a short walk, etc. Make sure those things are in place for when you need them.

Works Cited and Resources

Althen, Gary. 1995. *The Handbook of Foreign Student Advising*. Intercultural Press, Inc. Boston, Intercultural Press, Inc.

Ericksen, Robert. 2005. "Moving into Management: Assessing Your Readiness." Session presented October 12, 2005, Anaheim, California, at the NAFSA: Association of International Educators Region XII conference.

Fisher, Roger, William Ury, and Bruce Patton. 1991. *Getting to Yes: Negotiating Agreement without Giving In*, Second Edition. New York: Houghton Mifflin Company.

Hallett, Mark, Parandeh Kia, and Melinda Wood. 2001. "Planning Your Career Path in International Education." Presented November 2001, Palm Springs, California, at the NAFSA: Association of International Educators Region XII Conference.

Kruger, Justin and David Dunning. 1999. Unskilled and Unaware of It: How Difficulties in Recognizing One's Own Incompetence Lead to Inflated Self-Assessments. *Journal of Personality and Social Psychology*, Vol. 77, No. 6, p. 1121–1134.

Van de Water, Jack. 2006. "Lessons Learned: Musings on a 30-Year Career in International Education." *International Educator*, Vol. 15, No. 1, p. 57–61.

Young, Nancy E. "Navigating the Gray Zone: Decision Making in the International Office." Session presented May 27, 1999, Denver, Colorado, at the NAFSA: Association of International Educators Annual Conference.

YOUR NOTES

Appendix A

MAPPING YOUR CAREER PATH

As we indicated in Chapter 1, comparing job descriptions in international advising can help you understand your current position and where you might like to be in the future. The first matrix is designed to help you make these comparisons in an organized way. While this may seem like a mere matching up of job duties, it may reveal an "ah, ha!" or two for you as you think about what matters to you in your job and how you would like your career to evolve.

We encourage you to combine the "strategic planning" approach with the "serendipitous unfolding" approach to career planning. Feel free to borrow items from the sample job description for an international student adviser on page 8 in Chapter 1 as you do the first exercise and supplement it with other items as well.

The second matrix, designed to help with the same exercise, is likely to take on a completely different spin when you project your career five years out. Try it again, but with some modifications. If you don't feel that you're ready to plan that far ahead right now, come back and do this exercise in six months or a year from now.

Analysis of Current Position	Current Actual Job Duties	Ideal Job Description	Do I Have What I Need to Do This? What's the Plan for Getting It?	Do I Enjoy Doing This?
Cross-cultural skill building and training (for others)				
Immigration advising (with student/scholar interaction either online or in person)				
Immigration processing (data processing, record keeping, form production, etc.)				
Management and/or supervision (student help or other staff)				
Programming (activities, clubs, etc.)				
Working conditions (space, staffing, level of contact with students or scholars, salary, professional development opportunities)				
Other duties (as currently assigned or that you would like to be responsible for)				

Analysis of Position in the Future	What My Job Duties Will Probably Be in 5 Years If I Stay in This Position in This Office/Unit	Ideal Job Description for What I Would Like to Be Doing in 5 Years	What Will I Need to Do This? What's the Plan for Getting It?	Will I Want to Do This?
Cross-cultural skill building and training (for others)				
Immigration advising (with student/scholar interaction either online or in person)				
Immigration processing (data processing, record keeping, form production, etc.)				
Management and/or supervision (student help or other staff)				
Programming (activities, clubs, etc.)				
Working conditions (space, staffing, level of contact with students or scholars, salary, professional development opportunities)				
Other duties (as currently assigned or that you would like to be responsible for)				

YOUR NOTES

Appendix B

NAFSA CODE OF ETHICS

Members of NAFSA: Association of International Educators are dedicated to providing high-quality education and services to participants in international educational exchange. NAFSA members represent a wide variety of institutions, disciplines, and services. This Code of Ethics that proposes to set standards for the professional preparation and conduct of all NAFSA members must accommodate that diversity as well as emphasize common ethical practices. The Code sets forth rules for ethical conduct applicable to all NAFSA members. It does not provide a set of rules that prescribe how members should act in all situations. Specific applications of the Code must take into account the context in which it is being considered. In addition to this Code, NAFSA has also enacted guidelines for specific areas of Professional practice not applicable to all members. These guidelines are set forth in the Principles for International Educational Exchange. Individuals should recognize that professional practices in more than one area could apply to them.

Members are encouraged to use the Code of Ethics as an educational tool for working with other members and nonmembers of NAFSA.

All members, whether paid or unpaid for their work in international educational exchange, are expected to uphold professional standards.

International educators operate in complex environments, with legitimate and sometimes competing interests to satisfy. Ultimately, their concern must be to the long-term health of international educational exchange programs and participants.

Sorting through ethical dilemmas is often best done with help from others, either one's colleagues in the organization or experts in the subject-matter area.

1. NAFSA MEMBERS HAVE A RESPONSIBILITY TO:

a. Maintain high standards of professional conduct.
b. Follow ethical practices outlined in the Code of Ethics. Strive to follow the ethical practices outlined in the Principles for International Educational Exchange.
c. Balance the wants, needs, and requirements of program participants, institutional policies, laws, and sponsors. Members' ultimate concern must be the long-term well-being of international educational exchange programs and participants.
d. Resist pressures (personal, social, organizational, financial, and political) to use their influence inappropriately and refuse to allow selfaggrandizement or personal gain to influence their professional judgments.
e. Seek appropriate guidance and direction when faced with ethical dilemmas.
f. Make every effort to ensure that their services are offered only to individuals and organizations with a legitimate claim on these services.

Since members work in an area affected by rapid social, political, and economic changes, they must stay informed of current developments to be professionally competent.

2. IN THEIR PROFESSIONAL PREPARATION AND DEVELOPMENT, MEMBERS SHALL:

a. Accurately represent their areas of competence, education, training, and experience.
b. Recognize the limits of their expertise and confine themselves to performing duties for which they are properly educated, trained, and qualified, making referrals when situations are outside their area of competence.
c. Be informed of current developments in their fields, and ensure their continuing development and competence.
d. Stay abreast of laws and regulations that affect their clients.
e. Stay knowledgeable about world events that impact international educational program participants.
f. Stay knowledgeable about differences in cultural and value orientations.
g. Actively uphold NAFSA's Code of Ethics when practices that contravene it become evident.

One of the most challenging aspects of work in the field of educational exchange is balancing among the dictates of various cultures and value systems. Members must be aware of the influence that culture has had on their own values and habits and on the interpretations and judgments they make of the thoughts and habits of others.

Proselytizing is defined as unsolicited, coercive, manipulative and/or hidden persuasion that seeks to influence others to adopt another way of thinking, believing or behaving.

While enjoying interpersonal interactions with people from other cultures, members need to avoid situations in which their judgments may be, or appear to be, clouded because of personal relationships— either positive or negative ones.

Although a categorical ban on accepting gifts might be impractical for members who work with individuals representing cultures where the giving of gifts is important, members need to exercise caution in accepting gifts that might be intended to influence them.

Members' professional and ethical responsibilities extend beyond program participants to all individuals with whom they have interactions, whether they are prospective students and scholars, friends and relatives of program participants, or the general public.

Students and scholars often don't understand the processes and procedures for safe guarding their rights in the United States. Members should provide information about these or make referrals as appropriate.

Being tolerant and respectful of different behaviors and values among individuals who are culturally similar is often more difficult than being tolerant of those differences of people from other cultures. Nevertheless, members should make every effort to show their same-culture colleagues the respect they show their different-culture clients.

Just as they have duties to their clients, members have duties to their professional colleagues. When members accept responsibilities through NAFSA, *they should carry them out promptly.*

It is often tempting to overlook the long-term need for professional development in the press of daily business. Members must remain cognizant of the need for continuing professional development.

3. IN RELATIONSHIPS WITH STUDENTS, SCHOLARS, AND OTHERS MEMBERS SHALL:

a. Understand and protect the civil and human rights of all individuals.
b. Not discriminate with regard to race, color, national origin, ethnicity, sex, religion, sexual orientation, marital status, age, political opinion, immigration status, or disability.
c. Recognize their own cultural and value orientations and be aware of how those orientations affect their interactions with people from other cultures.
d. Demonstrate awareness of, sensitivity to, and respect for other educational systems, values, beliefs, and cultures.
e. Not exploit, threaten, coerce, or sexually harass others.
f. Not use one's position to proselytize.
g. Refrain from invoking governmental or institutional regulations in order to intimidate participants in matters not related to their status.
h. Maintain the confidentiality, integrity, and security of participants' records and of all communications with program participants. Members shall secure permission of the individuals before sharing information with others inside or outside the organization, unless disclosure is authorized by law or institutional policy or is mandated by previous arrangement.
i. Inform participants of their rights and responsibilities in the context of the institution and the community.
j. Respond to inquiries fairly, equitably, and professionally.
k. Provide accurate, complete, current, and unbiased information.
l. Refrain from becoming involved in personal relationships with students and scholars when such relationships might result in either the appearance or the fact of undue influence being exercised on the making of professional judgments.
m. Accept only gifts that are of nominal value and that do not seem intended to influence professional decisions, while remaining sensitive to the varying significance and implications of gifts in different cultures.
n. Identify and provide appropriate referrals for students or scholars who experience unusual levels of emotional difficulty.
o. Provide information, orientation, and support services needed to facilitate participants' adaptation to a new educational and cultural environment.

4. IN PROFESSIONAL RELATIONSHIPS, MEMBERS SHALL:

a. Show respect for the diversity of viewpoints among colleagues, just as they show respect for the diversity of viewpoints among their clients.
b. Refrain from unjustified or unseemly criticism of fellow members,
c. other programs, and other organizations.
d. Use their office, title, and professional associations only for the conduct of official business.
e. Uphold agreements when participating in joint activities and give due credit to collaborators for their contributions.
f. Carry out, in a timely and professional manner, any NAFSA responsibilities they agree to accept.

5. IN ADMINISTERING PROGRAMS, MEMBERS SHALL:

a. Clearly and accurately represent the identity of the organization and the goals, capabilities, and costs of programs.
b. Recruit individuals, paid and unpaid, who are qualified to offer the instruction or services promised, train and supervise them responsibly, and ensure by means of regular evaluation that they are performing acceptably and that the overall program is meeting its professed goals.
c. Encourage and support participation in professional development activities.
d. Strive to establish standards, activities, instruction, and fee structures that are appropriate and responsive to participant needs.
e. Provide appropriate orientation, materials, and on-going guidance for participants.
f. Provide appropriate opportunities for students and scholars to observe and to join in mutual inquiry into cultural difference
g. Take appropriate steps to enhance the safety and security of participants.
h. Strive to ensure that the practices of those with whom one contracts do conform with NAFSA's Code of Ethics and the Principles for International Educational Exchange.

6. IN MAKING PUBLIC STATEMENTS, MEMBERS SHALL:

a. Clearly distinguish, in both written and oral public statements, between their personal opinions and those opinions representing NAFSA, their own institutions, or other organizations.
b. Provide accurate, complete, current, and unbiased information.

Original text approved by the NAFSA *Board of Directors on May* 28, 1989.
Revisions approved by the NAFSA *Board of Directors in October* 1992, *and September* 2000.
Additional text changes adopted on March 13, 2002, *and March* 9, 2003.

Appendix C

UNAUTHORIZED PRACTICE OF LAW

As you have read the various scenarios dealing with knotty problems faced by international advisers, you may have developed a sense of some larger issues. One such issue is the delicate balance between doing the work that we are hired to do as advisers and overstepping our professional boundaries into matters that are not part of our adviser role. The following is a discussion of one critical area: "practicing law without a license" or "unauthorized practice of law." As you will see, this is a complicated exercise in definitions of terms and interpretation of regulations that is meant to apply in a completely different setting. In some ways, this discussion muddies the water—in others, it clears things up. That's why we have included it as an appendix.

Nearly all international advisers have been in a situation in which they are asked for legal advice by a student or scholar who just wants to know "a little something" about how some action or another might affect their status in the United States. Advisers often are asked questions such as "What are my immigration options if I get married to an American?," or "What would happen to my status if I was found guilty of a misdemeanor like drunk driving?"

Read this discussion carefully, then again read your job description and ask yourself about the boundaries it establishes. Does the information prompt you to discuss any changes with your supervisor or with your institution's Office of General Counsel? We expect that a better understanding of unauthorized practice of law will probably help you develop a different perspective about the kind of guidance that is appropriate for you to offer in your capacity as an international adviser.

Unauthorized practice of law (UPL) is a topic that is variously defined and hotly debated. The confusion that surrounds the topic is understandable because part of the definition is determined state by state. To add to the confusion, various government agencies have offered their opinions over the years. Periodically individual government officials put forth their ideas. Virtually every immigration attorney has thought about the topic. Every international adviser needs to give these ideas some careful consideration in defining his or her position.

People usually discuss UPL in the context of the "notario" or immigration practitioner who is a non-attorney but who provides immigration counseling for a fee. That arrangement presents its own interesting set of problems. But international advisers consider UPL in a different light and ask how they (as international student or scholar advisers) are affected by rulings on UPL. A variety of questions present themselves:

1. How is UPL defined?
2. Does where I live make a difference?
3. How does the Department of Homeland Security define UPL?
4. What kinds of trouble can I get into with UPL?
5. What kinds of trouble can my university get into with UPL?
6. Is this a tempest in a teapot?

Before seeking answers to these questions, a number of commonly accepted concepts regarding UPL and the work of international advisers are listed below.

- Unauthorized practice of law issues should be separated from competency issues. Just because you know how to do something doesn't mean that you should do it. Just because you don't know how to do something doesn't mean that you shouldn't learn how to do it and then do it well. Experienced international advisers know the limits of their own competence. They also know that the laws and regulations are not impossible to understand. It helps to have been to law school to understand legal language, but it's not necessary. UPL should NOT be defined as "anything I don't already know but guess at anyway."
- A college or university (like any other "person" in the law) has the option of operating pro se in legal matters. (A rough translation of pro se is "for oneself.") The university can speak for itself in all kinds of legal settings; immigration is one of those settings. The key point is that when the university is operating pro se, it represents only its own interests.
- DSO/RO (Designated School Official/Responsible Officer) duties are provided for in law and regulation. Any specific regulatory DSO or RO duty is, by definition, NOT unauthorized practice of law.
- Opinions are just opinions. You can have an opinion; we can have opinions. DHS officials can have opinions. Immigration attorneys can have opinions. Opinions do not have the power of law or regulation, but they are interesting, informative, and thought provoking.
- Any immigration advice by non-attorneys or nonauthorized representatives for a fee is UPL. This does not include our salaries; nor does it include a fee-for-service that our office may deem necessary. That money never comes directly to us as advisers. It goes to the college or university.

Our universities assign duties to us. We might be assigned to run an international student leadership group or to organize an international festival. Or we might be assigned to process immigration petitions for the university. It may be that our duties include complete processing of all items pertaining to immigration for incoming students and faculty.

These concepts provide the framework you need to fully understand the answers to the questions we just posed.

1. *How is* UPL *defined?*

   UPL is variously defined. There is no federal law that defines or prohibits UPL, although there is clear federal law dealing with fraud and misrepresentation in immigration matters. Many states have, however, defined UPL for their citizens. If you are curious about the definitions in your own state, consult with your university counsel. In some states the State Supreme Court has the authority to set standards of admission of attorneys to the bar and establishes standards for who can represent individuals in need. The term "representation" has special meaning in this context—it is more than just standing up and arguing the case in a court.

   8 CFR 292.1 contains an important discussion of representation before immigration courts. While international advisers seldom (if ever) are in such a position, it is useful to see that the DHS has provision for "reputable individuals" or "accredited representatives" before the immigration courts. In practice, these terms usually refer to a clergyman who might appear with an alien in court or an employee of an immigrants' rights group who is a trained specialist (albeit a non-attorney) in a particular aspect of immigration law. 8 CFR 292 covers other topics as well: discipline of attorneys and representatives, appearances, service upon and action by attorney or representative of record and interpretation.

2. *Does it matter where I live?*

   Yes, it does. UPL is a matter of state regulation. This is an area you may wish to discuss with your institutional counsel. It is also a valuable topic of conversation with the American Immigration Lawyers Association (AILA) chapter in your city or state.

3. *How does* DHS *define* UPL?

   DHS (including legacy INS) has offered a variety of opinions on UPL several times over the years. In 1992, then INS General Counsel Joseph Rees[1] issued a six-page legal opinion on UPL by visa consultants and other nonaccredited service providers. Of interest are the following definitions:

   - "practice" is defined as the act or acts of any person appearing in any case, either in person or through the preparation or filing of any brief or other document, paper, application, or petition on behalf of another person or client before or with the Service, or any officer of the Service of the Board of Immigration Appeals (BIA).
   - "preparation" is defined as the study of the facts of a case and the applicable laws, coupled with the giving of advice and auxiliary activities, including the incidental preparation of papers.

[1] Memorandum from Grover Joseph Rees III, INS General Counsel, issued June 9, 1992. Interpreter Releases, Vol. 69, No. 25, July 6, 1992, p. 823.

- The scope of the term "representation" is a very broad one. It includes activities that range from incidentally preparing papers for a person, to giving a person advice about his or her case, to appearing before DHS on behalf of a person. "Representation" does not extend to those services that consist only of assisting persons in completing preprinted Service forms. Therefore, a visa consultant or any other person who is not a licensed attorney or authorized representative pursuant to 8 CFR 292 will not be in violation of federal immigration regulations if he or she engages in these limited activities and receives either no remuneration or nominal remuneration.

In 1995, Doris Meissner, Commissioner of the INS, reflected on Service opinions of the past few years and offered this summary:

> The practice of law includes advising individuals concerning the selection, completion, and filing of Service forms, in addition to actually appearing before a Service officer.... Even advice limited to something as "simple" as selecting and completing the proper Service form constitutes the practice of law, since this advice depends on the legal conclusion that the client is eligible for the particular benefit.[2]

Note that this definition is in the context of offering such services for a fee.

4. *What kinds of trouble can I get into with* UPL?

   There are substantial penalties for fraud in an immigration setting. Details are available in a memorandum from INS General Counsel Paul Virtue[3] of September 3, 1997 that explains the IIRAIRA provisions for "falsely made applications." The key item for most international advisers is that they not offer their services for a fee. It is clearly UPL to charge for immigration advice if one is not an attorney or authorized representative.

5. *What kinds of trouble can my university get into with* UPL?

   If you are performing duties in which the university is operating pro se, there is no problem. There is a great deal more ambiguity in situations where there is no pro se element. You might want to look at your job description and discuss it with your supervisor and/or university counsel if it contains (or implies) duties that constitute representation of the alien, even though you do not charge the alien. Remember that you as an international adviser do not do these things for a fee from the alien, so you are not engaging in UPL as most people define it. But you might want to be clear about how much representation of the alien's interest you actually engage in. If you and your university counsel are satisfied that this is appropriate to your setting (and if there is no fee involved), you and your university are probably in the clear.

[2] Memorandum from Doris M. Meissner, INS Commissioner, to all INS offices, Practice of Law by Unlicensed "Immigration Brokers," File No. HQ 292-P (January 18, 1995), reported on and reproduced in 72 Interpreter Releases 529, 538 (April 17, 1995).

[3] Memorandum from Paul W. Virtue, Acting Executive Associate Commissioner, issued September 3, 1997. AILA InfoNet Doc. No. 99091790 (posted Sep. 17, 1997).

If you are a DSO or an RO/ARO for your institution, you have an obligation to abide by the laws and regulations that govern those programs. In fact, you affirm that you have read and understand those regulations when you take on those duties and become a signatory for the institution in these matters. To violate those provisions puts the F and/or J programs of your institution at risk.

If you file employment status applications (H or PR applications), you and your university counsel will also want to review your institution's level of compliance with provisions of those applications. There are serious penalties for willful noncompliance. Those penalties apply to the institution, not the individual. It would be a rare case that an institution would be a willful violator, but the penalties are serious for the institution. In the most extreme cases, the institution would be barred from issuing any immigration document for a period of time. It is well worth knowing the parameters in such matters.

6. *Is this a tempest in a teapot?*

   Yes and no. International advisers do not charge individuals for their services. But we do make assessments about individual cases. We do select which forms are appropriate in a given setting. We offer advice on how to complete immigration forms. It is sometimes true that we offer advice to aliens about immigration forms that pertain strictly to them and not with the university. An example of this is giving advice or assistance in filing an extension of stay form for family members where the university is filing an extension H-1B for an employee of the university. Failing or refusing to do so would be a professional omission as an employee of the institution and would create a very problematic situation for the alien and the university, especially if the family had to return home and the principle alien quit his/her university job. That's the critical link: you are serving your institution by meeting the relevant visa status issues of an employee's dependents. Nevertheless, international offices should discuss the scope of their activities with their general counsel so that this important ally is fully informed.

YOUR NOTES

Appendix D

ORGANIZING YOUR FOLLOW-UP ACTIVITIES

There are suggestions for Follow-Up Activities at the end of each chapter. For readers who prefer checklists or workbooks, we have rearranged the activities to give you another framework for developing your career plan. This is not meant to be an exhaustive list. Rather, it is a series of suggestions organized from those that can be done unobtrusively without involving other people (so are relatively "safe" activities for novice international advisers) to those that require consultation or interaction with others in a variety of more complex settings. Read through them and see what works for you.

One way to organize yourself would be to establish a one-year planning calendar. You can do this on a wall-mounted calendar or electronically, whatever you like. First, write in the events and activities that you know will affect your workload: new student orientation and registration, international fair planning, holidays, other staff members' vacations, and so on. Then write in any dates when your campus is closed or there are few people on campus. Finally, when you have a sense of your relatively less-busy times, begin to schedule the suggested activities. If it will take more than one year to do all of them, make this a multi-year commitment to yourself. We know from experience that if you don't put professional development and planning into your schedule ahead of time, the weeks and months will race by and you will fall behind on creating your own career pathway. Don't let that happen!

Phase I. Learning to Read the Existing Road Map

- Get to know what matters to you by using one of the self-assessment instruments mentioned in Chapter 1 (e.g., the Myers-Briggs Type® or the Strong Interest® Inventories).
- Investigate local/state professional networks.
- Check out the NAFSA Web site.
- Read one or two cross-cultural books.
- Investigate the Carnegie Foundation Web site and find your campus in the listings.
- Find out which Big Six associations your institution belongs to.
- Learn about the history of your campus.
- Read the campus newspaper.
- Get a copy of your campus strategic plan. Is there anything about "international" on it?
- Talk to your boss about town/gown relations in your community.
- Read the local newspaper.
- Order the NAFSA *Adviser's Manual*.

- Investigate the Web sites of DHS, SEVIS, and DOS. Bookmark what interests you and what you think you will regularly use.
- Go online and take a look at the structure of the Immigration and Nationality Act. You don't have to read it—just look at the structure.
- Get a copy of 8 CFR 214(f) and 22 CFR 62 and read them.
- Take a look at www.travel.state.gov. Find the section on wait times for visa appointments. Select ten cities where a lot of students or scholars at your institution come from and compare.
- Research the Web site for your city/county government. Note the names and contact information for the mayor and city council members.
- Research the Web site for your state legislature. Note the names and contact information for the people who represent where you live and where your campus is located.
- Research the Web sites for your Congressional delegation. Note the names and contact information for your two senators and the representatives for where you live and where your campus is located.
- Register to vote.
- Find out who on your campus is responsible for government relations.
- Read a couple of sample advocacy letters on the NAFSA Web site.
- Identify a mentor.

Phase II. Going Out for a Spin Around the Neighborhood

- See if you can get an organizational chart of the administration on your campus or at least for the unit in which your office resides. If it has no names (only positions) on it, cross-reference it with the campus phone directory.
- Secure a copy of your institution's financial report. It may be posted on the Web or you may need to ask your boss to help you locate it. Read it.
- Ask a faculty member you know if you can attend a departmental faculty meeting and then listen with cross-cultural ears.
- Attend a local meeting of a professional organization that will help develop your professional skills (e.g., NAFSA, NASPA).
- Participate in a tour of the nearest Port of Entry (POE) and USCIS facility; these are often arranged by a local professional group.
- Read the U.S. Immigration System chapter (currently Chapter 2) of the NAFSA *Adviser's Manual* and talk about it with your boss or a colleague.
- Investigate the Web sites for the three DHS branches that you need to interact with: USCIS, ICE, and CBP.

- Sign on to a professional listserv. Check the NAFSA Web site for resources.
- Accompany an international student or scholar on his/her visit to the Department of Motor Vehicles and the Social Security office.
- Read a cross-cultural book you like and discuss it with a colleague.
- If you have not already done so, participate in a couple of cross-cultural simulations games (e.g. BARNGA or BAFA BAFA) either on campus or at a conference. Compare the game with your own cross-cultural experiences.
- Write out a case study of a challenging situation you have dealt with.
- Develop a list of Web sites that you can hand to international students and scholars so that they can track their own immigration case or plan their next visa acquisition or sort out the procedures for getting a driver's license.
- Read the NAFSA Code of Ethics.
- Conduct an informational interview with one faith-based international student hospitality organization in your community.
- Establish an informational interview schedule for the next 6 months. The meetings don't need to be time consuming or expensive—they can be half-hour conversations over a cup of coffee. Examples of offices with whom you will want to establish relationships include: Registrar, Admissions, Financial Aid, Office of General Counsel, Office of Government and/or Community Relations, Office of Contracts and Grants, Human Resources Compensation Office, Human Resources Employment Office. You can make your own decisions on who to contact first. This activity may stretch over a couple of years.
- Make a list of potential programming partners across the campus as your network grows.
- Register to receive NAFSA Advocacy Alerts.
- Identify the reporters who cover the education "beat" for your local news media.
- Draft a practice advocacy letter. This is a letter that you write as a private citizen. Discuss your draft with a colleague.
- Study the positions of candidates for office and think about how you would vote in an election with specific international education issues in mind. These might include immigration, funding for higher education, or funding for medical research.

Phase III. *Charting Your Personal Path—Going the Distance*

- Discuss with colleagues one of the cross-cultural books or concepts you have encountered. Compare what you've read with your professional observations.
- Debrief with colleagues after you've shared a cross-cultural simulation experience. Discuss the relative merits and applicability of the experience. Compare what you've experienced with your observations of people who are actually encountering new cultures.
- Become a dues-paying member of a professional association.
- Help your local or regional professional group with identifying topics and setting the agenda for meetings.
- Attend a professional regional conference.
- Attend a professional national conference.
- Propose and deliver a session at one of these conferences.
- Seek funds for attending one of these professional development activities.
- Send an advocacy letter to an elected official. If sending electronically from your campus, consult with appropriate staff as discussed in Chapter 4.
- Continue to clarify your work values: what matters to you in terms of geography, type of institution, type of international office, and other work-related environmental factors.
- Establish a timeline for the progress of your career. Talk about it with a trusted friend, your mentor, your family, and others whose judgment you respect.